Voluptuous Yearnings

New Feminist Perspectives Series

General Editor: Rosemarie Tong, Davidson College

Claiming Reality: Phenomenology and Women's Experience
by Louise Levesque-Lopman, Regis College

Evidence on Her Own Behalf: Women's Narrative as Theological Voice
by Elizabeth Say, California State University, Northridge

Feminist Jurisprudence: The Difference Debate
Edited by Leslie Friedman Goldstein, University of Delaware

Is Women's Philosophy Possible?
by Nancy J. Holland, Hamline University

Manhood and Politics: A Feminist Reading of Political Theory
by Wendy L. Brown, University of California, Santa Cruz

Rethinking Ethics in the Midst of Violence: A Feminist Approach to Freedom
by Linda A. Bell, Georgia State University

Rethinking Masculinity: Philosophical Explorations in Light of Feminism
Edited by Larry May, Washington University, and Robert A. Strikwerda, Indiana University, Kokomo

Speaking from the Heart: A Feminist Perspective on Ethics
by Rita C. Manning, San Jose State University

Toward a Feminist Epistemology
by Jane Duran, University of California, Santa Barbara

Voluptuous Yearnings: A Feminist Theory of the Obscene
by Mary Caputi, Saint Mary's College

Women, Militarism, and War: Essays in History, Politics, and Social Theory
Edited by Jean Bethke Elshtain, Vanderbilt University, and Sheila Tobias, University of Arizona

Women, Sex, and the Law
by Rosemarie Tong, Davidson College

Voluptuous Yearnings

A Feminist Theory of the Obscene

Mary Caputi

Rowman & Littlefield Publishers, Inc.

ROWMAN & LITTLEFIELD PUBLISHERS, INC.

Published in the United States of America
by Rowman & Littlefield Publishers, Inc.
4720 Boston Way, Lanham, Maryland 20706
3 Henrietta Street
London WC2E 8LU, England

British Cataloging in Publication Information Available

Library of Congress Cataloging-in-Publication Data

Caputi, Mary.
Voluptuous yearnings : a feminist theory of the obscene / Mary
Caputi.
p.   cm. — (New feminist perspectives series)
Includes bibliographical references and index.
1. Pornography—Social aspects—United States. 2. Obscenity (Law)
3. Women—United States—Crimes against. 4. Feminism—United
States. 5. Feminist theory. I. Title. II. Series.
HQ472.U6C36 1993 363.4'7'0973—dc20 93-26056 CIP

ISBN 0-8476-7885-7 (cloth : alk. paper)
ISBN 0-8476-7886-5 (paper : alk. paper)

Printed in the United States of America

The paper used in this publication meets the minimum requirements of
American National Standard for Information Sciences—Permanence of
Paper for Printed Library Materials, ANSI Z39.48–1984.

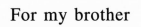
For my brother

Contents

Acknowledgments

I am deeply indebted to Susan Buck-Morss for her superb reading of this manuscript and invaluable contributions to it. I am grateful for her continued interest in my work. I owe a good deal, too, to Christine di Stefano and Kathleen Jones, who read the piece with care and commented at length. The following persons also contributed to it at various stages: Isaac Kramnick, Biddy Martin, Werner Dannhauser, Ann Clark, Ann Loux, Andrew Cutrofello, Dianne Rothleder, and Tom Parisi. I would also like to thank Jonathan Sisk, Lynn Gemmell, Rasha El-Ganzouri, Melissa Checots, and every member of my immediate family for their various forms of help, advice, support, and concern.

Feminism, Pornography, and the Obscene

In the United States, 1976 marked the inception of an impassioned feminist battle over pornography. In that year, members of Women Against Violence Against Women (WAVAW) in the Los Angeles area voiced their displeasure at a billboard displayed on Sunset Boulevard. This billboard advertised a recently released Rolling Stones album and depicted a woman bound, beaten, and covered with bruises; its caption read "I'm black and blue from the Rolling Stones and I love it." Angered by the misogynist implications of this advertisement, WAVAM defaced the placard and mounted a campaign to have it removed. They were successful.[1]

This incident hardly marked the first time that the media and other systems of representation had been scrutinized from a feminist vantage point: the National Organization of Women (NOW) had long made public its intentions to "protest, and endeavor to change, the false image of women now prevalent in the main media, and in the texts, ceremonies, laws and practices of our major social institutions."[2] Nevertheless, the event surrounding the Rolling Stones' advertisement proved significant in that it spurred many feminists to redouble their efforts in curtailing the preponderance of sexist imagery in the American media.

Amid the various critiques of advertising and its imagery, certain feminists chose to focus their attention on one specific, highly charged form of representation: pornography. This genre deserved special attention, it was felt, because it encapsulates the nexus of power relations surrounding gender and sexuality as conceived within our culture. Although very divided among themselves as to what

1

pornography is, how it operates, and why it is objectionable, feminists critical of this form of representation nevertheless agree that pornographic imagery distills the archeplot of power relations[3] prevailing between the sexes. While this genre is seemingly about pleasure alone, they contend, it is also about power and the social inequality of the sexes.

Particularly objectionable to antipornography feminists, then, is the tendency of some sexually explicit imagery to reproduce and seemingly endorse an Aristotelian understanding of gender relations. This understanding clings to a teleological interpretation of implicit ends; it argues that there is resonance between nature and culture, between the world's material givens and its social, political, and economic arrangements, between the human body and the social construction of gender. Arguing in support of natural hierarchies, this ideology posits men as knowing, thinking, acting human subjects, the makers of history, the philosophers of life. In contrast, women are essentially matter, passive receptacles waiting to be filled according to an androcentric ethos; they are more body than mind and thus embrace whatever ideological role patriarchy assigns them. Hence it is argued that pornography appealing to a male audience presupposes a certain subject-object relationship: the subject is a male actor/consumer/viewer, the object a female body-on-display.[4] This belief in man-as-mind (subject), woman-as-matter (object) of course buttresses the status quo.

Arguing that pornography underwrites traditional masculine and feminine realms hardly exhausts the battery of criticisms feminists register against this genre. Indeed, following the Sunset Boulevard incident, the feminist antipornography campaign proliferated along various institutional and theoretical lines. The debate over this system of representation has caused philosophical differences among feminists to emerge: radical and marxist feminists, libertarians, and sex radicals constitute several major camps, each with a different understanding of human sexuality and of the manner in which it informs a feminist analysis.[5] However, the cited analysis concerning a cultural archeplot of power is significant in that it informs so many feminist criticisms of pornography; it certainly forms the pillar upon which the radical feminist critique—of particular interest to this investigation—rests.

Of course, the question of what constitutes objectionable expression is of interest not only to feminists, it remains a hotly debated issue in American political and cultural life. In the late 1980s and early 1990s, we have witnessed many debates to this effect, debates seeking to clarify, define, and bring closure to the problems surrounding objectionable expression. Stated more broadly, we have seen a groundswell of interest in a topic that by its very nature promises to spark controversy in a society so committed to free expression: namely, the topic of obscenity.[6]

American Conservatism and Artistic Expression: The Politics of the Obscene

Controversies surrounding this issue have been especially manifest in the art and music worlds. For instance, several years ago the National Endowment for the Arts found itself at the center of a heated political debate focused upon federal funding of the arts. This debate was underway by the late 1980s due to a grant awarded to photographer Andres Serrano; his work includes the controversial *Piss Christ*, which shows a crucifix submerged in urine. However, it was the bold, some would argue brazen, homoerotic photographs of Robert Mapplethorpe which truly garnered this issue national attention. The debate asked whether federal money should support art exhibits that some people deem morally objectionable. This discussion hinged not only on the politics surrounding who makes these decisions but on the long-standing question of what distinguishes erotic art from obscenity. Many felt that the homoeroticism of Mapplethorpe's work categorized it as obscene; consequently, they argued that as unprotected speech it should be denied funding. Those urging this denial of funding, among them the outspoken Senator Jesse Helms, thus focused on what they deemed to be the controversial subject of Mapplethorpe's art. Conversely, people supporting Mapplethorpe's freedom of expression, favoring continued and unfettered federal funding for the NEA, maintained that the photographs in question clearly possessed serious artistic merit and were categorically not obscene. Moreover, they claimed that in fact homophobia, bigotry, and a fundamental conservatism underlay this debate, which in truth was only superficially about obscenity. Despite several lawsuits, that particular controversy was resolved in favor of continued NEA funding, to proceed uninhibited by closer governmental supervision: federal money for artistic expression cannot be earmarked.[7] Even the conservative President Bush offered support of artists' freedom at a White House press conference: "I don't know of anybody in the government that should be set up to censor what you write or what you paint or how you express yourselves . . . I'm against censorship."[8]

Several months later, charges of obscenity were again brought to the artistic community. This time, the charges targeted the black rap group 2 Live Crew. It was argued that songs included on the group's album, *As Nasty As They Wanna Be*, contained language and statements of a highly objectionable nature, so much so that a Florida judge ruled the lyrics obscene and banned the album's sale in that state. Not the first time that contemporary music had been condemned as distasteful or unethical—similar charges had been registered against Ozzy Ozbourne and Judas Priest—this incident generated tremendous controversy given the issues of race and class that rap music typically stresses. Indeed, those opposed to the album's banning maintained that obscenity was not the real issue, but rather a red herring used to mask an underlying bigotry pervasive in American culture. This counterargument insisted that white rock musicians, especially heavy metal bands, frequently use language and imagery easily as risqué as those employed by 2 Live Crew. Hence it was surmised that in banning the album, the Florida courts expressed racism rather than a desire to maintain high standards of public decency and artistic merit. The arguments used to defend 2 Live Crew thus parallel the defenses of Robert Mapplethorpe's art: What masquerades as a debate about obscenity merely disguises a more deep-seated struggle between white, mainstream America and marginalized groups challenging the former's position of power.[9]

Thus in contemporary American society, accusations of sexism, homophobia, racism, and class politics have entered the fray where the topic of obscenity is concerned. Understandably, the debates have remained very political, focused less on the basic concept of obscenity than on the politics surrounding its cultural manifestations. In short, the debates have not asked "What is obscenity?" but "Who controls artistic expression?" These two questions are interrelated; I would argue that the first, the more theoretical, warrants further elaboration.

Rather than immediately enter the political fray, then, I wish to first ask why obscenity stirs such deep emotions. We treat it as a political and legal issue necessarily ensconced within larger agendas. Yet rarely do we delve deeply into its theoretical standing, asking more broadly: What is it? This is because obscenity represents primarily an emotional issue, one whose equivocal nature can infuriate and enrage, and which penetrates to the deepest level of our psyche. We don't just look away, refuse to buy an album, or choose not to see a film. We argue, condemn, censor, applaud, and support. Indeed, it is my conviction that the specific characteristics of the above-mentioned arguments have not themselves accounted for the intensity of the debates. It is not the feminism, identity politics, marxism, radicalism, or libertarianism of the positions that ensures a spirited discussion. Rather, it is the centrality of obscenity at all that guarantees such arguments will be vehement, the convictions supporting them ironclad. Therefore, it is only after we address obscenity's theoretical underpinnings that we can scrutinize the politics involved. What then is obscenity?

Obscenity: Continuity, Communion, Fusion

Obscenity incorporates transgression and taboo, the violation of boundaries, the exceeding of subconsciously consensual limits.[10] In this, it is integral to our culture, and perhaps to all cultures. My central argument in these pages is that obscenity constitutes an especially important category in the contemporary industrialized West. This is because it highlights the distinction between the domain of everyday life—the intelligible, orderly world of rationality, progress, technology, and the Freudian reality principle—and the dionysian realm of irrational abandon, the absence of self, transgression of boundaries, communion, and even fusion. Largely sexual, scatological, and eschatological, obscenity combines our immediate impulse for pleasure with a deeper, more complicated desire—to be explained later in terms of human drives, a high level of repression, and alienation—to bypass our socially imposed boundaries and apprehend a psychic death. Obscenity is essential to culture because it calls into question the limits of that culture, unmasking our impulse to transgress, even deny, the orderly realm and to be in contact with something both primally within us and necessarily beyond our reach. In obscene expression, we both uncover and rediscover an unmediated, "bodily" relationship to reality.

Obscenity thus bears directly on the distinction between the sanctioned and unsanctioned realms of human experience. More important, this distinction not only keeps life well ordered, civil, and predictable, it also assures us that there exists a realm of being and of meaning beyond the everyday, beyond the commonplace, beyond the temperate and the socially conditioned.

Without the possibility of transgressing our discrete limits, of appreciating the fluid, fictitious nature of our imposed identities, life assumes a jejune, shallow quality; we lack "an erotic sense of reality."[11]

I thus understand the obscene as that dimension of culture that allows us to cross boundaries, exceed limits, apprehend the irrational, and experience the dialectic between life and death. It encourages us to lose touch with the delimited identities we assume in daily life and bespeaks the interconnected fear and desire that encourage us to go beyond, to leave behind our rational selves and experience "continuity" rather than "discontinuity." "Continuity" refers to the annihilation of the distinctions between self and other, between self and the world. With continuity, we no longer claim the delimited ego boundaries characteristic of "discontinuity," which correspond to our discrete, given identities. Hence the obscene causes us to experience the dialectic between being and nonbeing. We are disburdened of the tensions that necessarily inform our existence as distinct selves, and undergo a kind of psychic death. In this, obscenity puts into play our sense of the primal, the archaic, and the unmediated so lacking in our culture. Roman Polanski's *Repulsion* dramatizes how the obscene is imbued with a sense of the primal. When a young woman learns of her sister's sexual experiences, she becomes upset. From her window, she can see a convent across the street, yet all she seems to hear are the sounds of her sister's lovemaking emanating from a nearby bedroom. Her state of emotional disturbance leads to an obsession with meat. As she gradually descends into mental illness, she acquires the habit of carrying pieces of unwrapped meat in her handbag for days at a time.

Obscenity thus challenges the accepted limits of culture, not always with a view toward redefining these limits but toward revisiting their reasons for being, and toward underscoring their ultimate tenuousness. In allowing the dialectical nature of the human impulses to emerge—what classical psychoanalysis terms the admixture of the erotic and death drives—obscene materials allow for an undifferentiated experience of the world, one in which ego boundaries have been loosened and the self forgotten. In sum, obscenity allows for continuity, the sensation of merging and fusion with the world, a sense of communion. It has already been observed by several authors that the obscene is thus heir to the religious traditions of sacrifice, resurrection, communion, and transubstantiation; Georges Bataille, Jessica Benjamin, and Susan Sontag have clearly articulated this point.[12]

Similarly, these pages will insist that religion and obscenity parallel one another in that both allow the truly dialectical nature of human existence to be put into play: clearly ascesis and orgasm are in some ways alike. Bernini's famous statue of *Saint Theresa and the Angel*, displayed at Santa Maria della Vittoria church in Rome, aptly portrays how the experience of God parallels one of sexual climax. In a moment of spiritual intensity, the saint reclines peacefully, head back, eyes closed, mouth ajar. She appears to be experiencing ecstacy, a sense of plenitude and culmination. Is she rejoicing in or transgressing from her saintly calling? Similarly, the rock star Madonna has been gifted with an intuitive sense of how spirituality and sexual impulse interconnect. In a 1989 interview, she explained that her "Like A Prayer" video portrays a woman who "reaches an orgasmic crescendo of sexual fulfillment intertwined with her love of God."[13] And the novel *The Story of O* recounts how a masochistic woman experiences joyful self-annihilation in relinquishing herself entirely to her sadistic suitors:

> Beneath the gazes, beneath the hands, beneath the sexes that defiled her, the whips that rent her, she lost herself in a delirious absence from herself which restored her to love and, perhaps, brought her to the edge of death. She was anyone, anyone at all. . . . (She felt) . . . as though she existed only in another life and perhaps did not really exist at all.[14]

Hence in promising the transgression of individual boundaries, obscenity affirms rather than dismisses the need for taboo. Without limits to surpass, there would be no sense of the beyond.

What distinguishes licit from illicit forms of experience and expression, turning the sexual, the scatological, and the eschatological into the obscene? It is obscenity's added insistence on the transgression of boundaries, its affirmation of the distinction between an accepted human sensibility—for instance, consensual sex—and that which truly offends, shocks, or fascinates. We recognize the obscene in its determined violation of established norms, its eagerness to proclaim from beyond the acceptable, its appeal to the uncanny. In fact, obscenity not only presupposes a distinction between the licit and illicit realms but depends on this distinction for its own appeal. Only if the boundary is real can we transgress it. Obscene expres-

sion bespeaks the desire to be assured that such boundaries are
genuine, that the difference between the intelligible and unintelligi-
ble realms is real, yet also that the two can and must coexist. Hence
obscenity underscores the function of cultural norms, necessarily
calling into question the threshold that delineates the accepted from
the perverse. Freud, discussed in detail later, posits that all civi-
lized human beings internalize such a threshold, which both ensures
their psychic repression and allows for civilization. Only if we or-
ganize, deny, and repress certain impulses can we proceed as a
human culture. For him, taboo lies at the bedrock of civilization,
enmeshed in our very drives. Thus obscenity—which draws attention to taboo and thereby challenges the limits of culture—delves
deeply into the human psyche. Is it any wonder that it gives rise to
such impassioned debates?

My reading of the obscene renders the quest for "sexual liberation" somewhat farcical and misdirected, for I interpret sexuality
as essentially alloyed with taboo. Albeit from a different theoretical standpoint, my reading of this topic joins in the Foucauldian
claim that to speak incessantly about sexual liberation is to announce
one's preoccupation with, and hence enslavement to, sexual standards and restraints. To announce one's sexual freedom, then, is to
announce one's awareness of sexual mores. Indeed, such a reading
reformulates the problem of lascivious expression, for even as, say,
pornography appeals to sexual agency and exploration, it necessarily reconfirms the presence of taboo in our culture. This genre depends upon subconsciously consensual limits in order to transgress
them; this is what makes it sell. Hence pornography's efforts to defy
prohibitions while relying on them to create titillation only emphasize their presence and power. I agree with Joel Kovel that, because
sexuality and sexually explicit materials always bespeak prohibition,
neither can fully submit to the unconflicted realm of *logos*, the realm
wherein all contradictions are resolved, all tensions dissolved, and
all things made rational, nameable, and accessible to human apprehension.[15] "Sexuality will always be accompanied by lines to cross,"
he writes, "and on the other side will lie the possibility of shame."[16]
Thus contrary to libertarian claims, sexuality always holds the potential to evoke shame; why else would "[o]ne of the essential features of pornography (be) the Commandment: 'Thou shalt not be
ashamed'"?[17] Obscene materials always dramatize the extent to
which we are not free from cultural prohibition.

In these pages, I in no way mean to imply that Western culture is insufficiently ashamed of its sexual mores. My argument is not that we need more guilt or that we are insufficiently restrained. Rather, I hope to demonstrate how integral obscenity is to culture. I hope to illustrate why we prefer clearly defined boundaries denoting what is and is not illicit, what scandalizes and disgraces, what qualifies as beyond the pale: this despite our hue and cry about sexual liberation, sexual identity, and the fulfillment promised by orgasm. This exposition on obscenity's integral status will then yield an explanation as to why this topic is currently of such interest in American culture.

The Absence of Continuity in Western Culture

My argument is foregrounded in the assertion that the experience and indeed entire concept of continuity is generally lacking from contemporary Western culture. The reasons for this are numerous and complex, and I would not pretend to be able to explain this phenomenon fully. However, I contend that certain hallmarks of twentieth-century, industrialized Western society contribute to this specific lack in human experience, a lack to which the obscene responds. Most prominent among these hallmarks, of course, is the ideology of secular humanism, aligned as it is with the realm of *logos*, rationalism, individualism, human progress, and capitalism.

Secular humanism promises to deliver a society that is technologically advanced, efficient, rational, catering to human need, and comfortable. And in good measure, it has done so. Yet hasn't it also produced the obverse? Aren't there striking ways in which Western capitalist culture is irrational, unaligned with human need and proportion, unfit for human life? The writings of Frankfurt Institute intellectuals and other critical theorists have eloquently addressed capitalism's paradoxical tendency to alienate human beings from themselves and one another even as it putatively advances the humanist tradition. Reason, progress, technology, science: Ironically, these and other tenets of Enlightenment philosophy thwart rather than champion our humanity when pursued exclusively. Enlightenment rationality embodies a dialectic that turns back on itself; attempts to bring all facets of human life and the body under the aegis of *logos* proves reductionist and distorting. Hence, in *The Dialectic of Enlightenment*, Max Horkheimer and Theodor Adorno write:

> In the most general sense of progressive thought, the Enlightenment
> has always aimed at liberating men from fear and establishing their
> sovereignty. Yet the fully enlightened earth radiates disaster trium-
> phant. The program of the Enlightenment was the dissolution of myths
> and the substitution of knowledge for fancy. . . . Power and knowl-
> edge are synonymous. . . . There is to be no mystery—which means,
> too, no wish to reveal mystery.[18]

Certainly those scholars associated with the Frankfurt School
and other critical theorists are not alone in linking capitalism to
human alienation given the violences of Enlightenment rationality
and dehumanizing aspects of our material conditions. Yet their texts
on this topic, to be discussed presently, are among the most re-
nowned.

Secular humanism, which I argue discourages continuity in our
culture, also finds expression in the doctrine of classical liberalism.
This political theory so prevalent in the West similarly privileges
individuality, abstract reason, progress, and technology over a more
collectivist notion of social order and the social good. Integral to
the tradition of secular humanism, classical liberalism originally
sought to displace certain tenets of the ancien régime—its emotional ties to the monarchy, an acceptance of class relations and social
hierarchy, a religiosity that squelched political dissension—and in-
troduce a rational positivism in their place. Hence we witness the
significant epistemological shift in the direction of science and
empiricism that typifies modernity, a shift that I would argue has
encouraged the gradual but significant eclipse of intuition and a
dialectical, poetic sense of reality in favor of knowledge and information. The impact of this eclipse—especially as it privileges instrumental rationality over dialectical thought—cannot be too broadly
stated. It is the most salient aspect of the secular humanist tradition
that has prevailed as the leading intellectual and cultural paradigm
since the Enlightenment. For example, as a culture, we no longer
see God in nature but view the latter entirely in terms of our own
mastery and agency. We understand nature not in relation to human
stewardship but as bearing the imprint of human authorship. Hence
Greenpeace and the Sierra Club are viewed as special interest groups,
their ethos falling outside the parameters of mainstream American
culture.

Of course, many intellectual paradigms take issue with secular
humanism. For instance, critical theory, feminism, psychoanalysis,

and deconstruction all thwart various humanist premises. The reigning postmodernist paradigm also partakes of this enterprise by acknowledging a decentered human subject for whom meaning is discursively produced rather than fixed, centered, or ontologically given. This theoretical rejection of *logos* subsequently causes meaning to resist closure and allows for free play in the relationship between signifier and signified. In its rejection of Enlightenment premises, this paradigm formulates a deliberate and substantial break from the humanist tradition. However, I would here like to focus on one way in which much contemporary theory has *not* redirected the Enlightenment's trajectory: It further discredits the continuous realm. Most importantly, I choose to emphasize how the cumulative spiritual and intellectual disarrangements that typify modernity and postmodernity *privatize* meaning, reschematizing and problematizing the question of human identity. This privatization of meaning naturally brings increased importance to the discontinuous realm, wherein we experience the world as differentiated, private beings concerned with our individual identities. My argument will be that this movement away from continuity toward discontinuity also brings unbearable pressures and anxieties to the latter realm. This gives rise to increased tension surrounding discontinuity, especially where sexuality is concerned. I wish to show that in the absence of continuity our culture seeks relief in such things as obscenity.

There are other factors, too, that contribute to the intellectual, emotional, and spiritual shift I have described; I cannot pretend to name them all. Suffice it to say that contemporary Western culture is marked by an individualistic, secular ethos that contributes to our inability to sustain the paradox between continuity and discontinuity. I would argue that this ethos displaces the tensions that inhere between these two domains onto the realm of discontinuity: what could remain dialectical instead expects closure. Hence I agree with Jessica Benjamin's observation that "we are facing unbearably intensified privatization and discontinuity, unrelieved by expressions of continuity."[19] We come to expect too much from our privatized identities, especially our sexual identities, subsequently characterized by anguish and even despair. I maintain that our concern with sexual freedom, identity, and fulfillment is not solely about sexuality but about the need to transcend delimited boundaries and experience continuity. Our preoccupation with sexuality reveals the need to rediscover the dialectic between being and nonbeing, to sustain the paradox between our life and death impulses. This human need

for the retreat from boundaries and (re)discovery of an unmediated
sense of reality clarifies why the topic of obscenity strikes deep
chords within our culture, why it stirs deep emotions.

Feminist Readings of Pornography
Encapsulate This Dialectic

Certain feminist analyses of pornography best encapsulate what
is at issue with obscenity: the human desire for an unmediated relationship to the world and to meaning. In these pages, I ferret out
specific feminist critiques of pornography because I feel they address our topic directly. Interestingly, these critiques have labelled
pornography "objectionable" but never "obscene"; this is because
most pornography, technically, counts as protected speech, the criteria of which I discuss in the next chapter. How, then, can a feminist analysis of pornography explain the human need for the obscene? The answer lies in the metaphorical feminine or maternal,
so central to certain feminist readings of pornography. Indeed, I hope
to illustrate how those feminist readings of pornography that rely
on the feminine-as-metaphor resonate with the themes of continuity
and discontinuity in our culture. In this, they uncover what is truly
at stake with obscenity.

Let me be clear that, in thus limiting myself, I in no way mean
to privilege the accusations registered by feminists above those articulated by others concerned with obscenity; my focus on the objectification of women does not contain the hidden agenda of over-
riding the charges of homophobia, racism, and class politics; nor
does it suggest that the concern over artistic freedom in the United
States is unfounded. I do not wish to imply that the charge of sexism, although important and very real, carries more political and
intellectual weight than these other complaints; nor do I intend to
diminish or overshadow other political issues at stake in various
obscenity debates currently underway. Instead, my focus on certain
feminist readings of pornography is meant to illustrate how these
readings direct us precipitously toward what is central to the obscene.

At the outset, I wish to make plain that my argument relies on
Freudian drive theory. This theory—criticized as vague, unscientif-
ic, and inadequately developed[20]—posits a dualism between the life
and death impulses, termed eros and thanatos. The former strives

to preserve the living organism and is forward-moving; the latter seeks to dissolve any connection to other beings, desires the absence of all tension, and strives to return the living organism to an inorganic state. Whereas eros seeks interraction, thanatos longs for calm homeostasis, a state in which the individual need not exert emotional or psychic energy. Both drives are understood as innate in all human beings, although many hold that the nature of social organization, and hence level of psychic repression, influences how we experience them.[21] Within these pages, I subscribe to the Freudian premise of drive theory, tempered by a critique of the social setting in which these drives are experienced.

My reliance on Freud's theory becomes complicated to the extent that I also employ Michel Foucault's now-celebrated analysis of discourse, sexuality, and power. Foucault, of course, in no way bows to the paradigms deployed by psychoanalysis. He argues that "the least glimmer of truth (about sexuality) is conditioned by politics."[22] Foucault thus strives to dismantle the privilege that psychoanalysis enjoys and to unmask the authority that it presumes; as a discourse, Foucault says, psychoanalysis merely keeps us worried about our "sex lives," self-policing, self-censoring, eager to conform to an essentially conservative ideology upholding a jealously guarded state. At the appropriate time, I hope to make clear how the writings of Freud and Foucault can in fact combine effectively in an analysis of obscenity.

Let me begin by explaining why I think certain feminist critiques of pornography—which incorporate the metaphorical feminine—prove especially important to an investigation into the obscene.

CHAPTER ONE

Metonymy and Fragmentation: Feminist Readings of Pornography

In order to allow the feminist critique of pornography to shed light on the general topic of obscenity, it is necessary first to consider how, from a feminist perspective, pornography issues objectionable statements, how it subtly imparts misogynist sensibilities. For if this system of representation accomplishes objectification via its display of unclothed women, we must ask what precludes *any* depiction of female nudity from doing the same. What separates pornography from less objectionable portrayals of human nakedness, for instance, the classical and neo-classical nude? After all, on one level, aren't the *Playboy* centerfold and Venus de Milo the same, aren't they both naked women? This question forces a more specific analysis of the claim that pornography reproduces the cultural archeplot that certain feminists deplore.

In these pages, I concern myself almost exclusively with the pictorial pornography consumed by heterosexual men. While other forms of this genre exist—for instance, pornography that is written or spoken (as in Dial-A-Porn), pictorial gay and lesbian pornography, and pornography that appeals to heterosexual women—here I analyze the visual display of nude women appealing to male heterosexuals. Like all pictorial pornography, this particular system of representation caters to voyeuristic impulses; it appeals to the pleasure in looking. Given this genre's insistence on the visual, then, a feminist critique of the male gaze necessitates an unraveling of those meanings with which our culture imbues the female body and its public display. The ideological implications and profoundly political statements that feminists identify in pornography thus emanate from its seemingly straightforward revelation of the unclothed human body. How can something so immediate be so politically charged?

The Radical Feminist Critique of Pornography: The Politics of the Gaze

There are numerous feminist readings of pornography, many of which stand in disagreement. As stated earlier, however, a number of feminists taking issue with this system of representation agree that it incorporates a pernicious sexual politics; certainly this is true of the radical feminist position exemplified in the writings of Andrea Dworkin, Susanne Kappeler, and Catharine MacKinnon, among others.[1] Their overarching criticism targets this genre's reproduction and seeming endorsement of the archeplot they seek to discredit: namely, the cultural privileging of men over women, a privileging that casts the former as human subjects, the latter as objects. Amid analyses of pictorial pornography catering to heterosexual men, antipornography feminists claim that this visual system of representation is rife with the implication that human subjectivity is reserved for men. In the Aristotelian tradition, men are transcendent subjects, thinkers, knowers, and actors; they are aligned with the idea (*morphe*). Conversely, women are essentially objects, immanent beings uninvolved in the realm of ideas; they are aligned with matter (*hyle*).[2] Male agency determines, acts upon, and consumes female objectivity; hence men bring form and meaning to the female realm of simple matter. Pornography thus subtly imparts the statement that men are active, thinking subjects and women passive, receptive objects. Men consume pornography and gaze at the female body; women pose for the camera. In thus feeding a male appetite by catering to masculine sensibilities, this genre reinforces the subject/object dynamic that informs gender relations: it does contain an ideology, one that is androcentric and status quo. Catharine MacKinnon dispels the claim that pornography simply produces titillation:

[P]ornography institutionalizes the sexuality of male supremacy, which fuses the erotization of dominance and submission with the social construction of male and female. Gender is sexual. Pornography constitutes the meaning of that sexuality. Men treat women as who they see women as being. Pornography constructs who that is. Men's power over women means that the way men see women defines who women can be. Pornography is that way.[3]

MacKinnon thus recognizes pornography's subtle fusion of sexual and ideological issues, a fusion that perpetuates a system of gender hierarchy. To her, pornography is "a practice of sexual politics, an institution of gender inequality."[4] According to many radical feminists, then, the ideology of pornography is objectionable in that it elides female subjectivity. Andrea Dworkin asks:

> And what is the value of this sexual object to men, since it is they who form her, use her, and give her what value she has? . . . [T]he female is the instrument; the male is the center of sensibility and power. . . . The object's purpose is to be the means by which the lover, the male, experiences himself: his desire. . . . The object, the woman, goes out into the world formed as men have formed her to be used as men wish to use her.[5]

Those opposed to this genre thus insist that it so reproduces, endorses, and applauds a male-subject/female-object dynamic as to be pernicious. These critics challenge the claim that pornography concerns itself exclusively with sex, that the implications with which it is replete are purely sexual. On the contrary, pornography is political, they argue, and insidiously defends a status quo that presupposes an androcentric point of reference. The pornographic "engagement depends upon the spectator's seeing the woman in the picture as other, as a fit object of investigation-by-scrutiny," writes Annette Kuhn; "[t]o this extent, it is a masculine engagement. . . . The photograph speaks to a masculine subject."[6] Photographs of nude females thus utter a host of statements about gendered cultural stereotypes, and the power relations that prevail between them. Kappeler states this broadly, insisting that pornography lays bare not only human bodies but an entire cultural archeplot: "The pornographic scenario is but a stark representation of the cultural position of the male gender vis-à-vis the female gender. . . . The archeplot has the structure Subject-verb-object, and the verb is transitive, always."[7]

The philosophic underpinnings of pornographic representation are thus commensurate with a notion of natural hierarchy and teleologically ordained power relations. It is to these underpinnings that feminists object. They do not take issue with pornography's sexual explicitness, its appeal to brute bodily impulse, or its bawdiness.

Rather, their critique is fueled by an analysis of power. It is therefore empirical: Pornography "is political, a political act in the real
world." Construing it as devoid of ideological implications itself
represents "a political conception, an ideological cornerstone of
patriarchal culture."[8] There exists a correlation between men, wom-
en, and the pornographic scenario; there is a relationship between
the empirical world of gendered subjects and the private world of
fantasy and desire to which pornography presumably responds. John
Berger writes of this ideology that, so insidious as to be almost
imperceptible, is internalized by women themselves:

> Men survey women before treating them. Consequently how a woman
> appears to a man can determine how she will be treated. To acquire
> some control over this process, women must contain it and interiorize
> it. . . . One might simplify this by saying: *men act* and *women appear.*
> Men look at women. Women watch themselves being looked at. This
> determines not only most relations between men and women but also
> the relation of women to themselves. The surveyor of woman in her-
> self is male: the surveyed female. Thus she turns herself into an object—
> and most particularly an object of vision: a sight.[9]

In keeping with the politics of the gaze, Berger insists, women
"are there to feed an appetite, not to have any of their own."[10]

Fragmentation: Female
Sexuality Equals Femininity

But the analysis extends further, to the viewer's obsession with
specific female bodily parts. Certain feminists understand this obsession not as a mere putting into play of sexual difference but as
an intended fragmentation of the woman to whom these parts belong. MacKinnon, Dworkin, Kuhn, Helen Longino,[11] Alan Soble, and
others have described this visual fragmenting of the female form
as highly objectionable, not because it indiscreetly displays bodily
parts that are typically concealed but because of the pernicious
implications that accompany this process. Specifically, these authors
maintain that pornography's fragmentation equates women with their
distinctly female bodily parts. "The cumulative message is that a
woman is only the sum of her parts," writes Soble.[12] Moreover, these
critics claim that pornography does not merely enhance these female features but presents them in such a way that they stand in

for the woman to whom they belong: they become a form of short-hand for the woman herself. Accordingly, the pornographic scenario imparts the statement, not that women have certain features, but that they *are* those features. Pornography equates female humanity with the female body, its critics contend, and with the sexual appeal of that body. In Kuhn's words, "[t]he vagina in the picture stands in for the enigma of the feminine."[13] This tendency to equate all of femininity with female sexuality is what distinguishes pornographic from other nude portrayals of the human figure. Pornographic images are objectifying, but also fragmenting of women: they display the female body in such a way that it becomes equated with the woman herself.

This metonymic dimension of pornography is important to our analysis. The ideas expressed in these pages uphold the conviction that pornography bespeaks the need to render a woman reifiable, something that can be hypostatized. As she becomes hypostatized, the aesthetic, sexual appeal of her body determines her overall value. Accordingly, if her looks readily inspire titillation, she is deemed valuable. This is a way of saying that women exist for one purpose: to produce erections.

Bernardo Bertolucci's *Last Tango in Paris* makes reference to this dehumanization of women, metonymically collapsible into bodily parts. Its protagonist, Paul, is thoroughly disenchanted with the materialist, hypocritical sensibilities of bourgeois culture. He feels that it overvalues form, convention, and protocol; everything is false, an arena for display, a scramble to look good. Throughout the film Paul seeks to convince his lover, Jeanne, of the hypocrisy, bigotry, and misogyny of bourgeois society. When she reminisces about her father the colonel, he retorts: "All uniforms are bullshit." When she insists that she had a "beautiful" childhood, he asks: "Is it beautiful to be made into a tattletale, to be forced to admire authority, or sell yourself for a piece of candy?" In this endeavor, Paul acts with a sense of urgency in light of Jeanne's impending marriage to Tom, a filmmaker. Hardly a disinterested observer, Paul intuitively feels that Jeanne's fiancé subscribes to a voyeuristic, misogynist ideology, one that delights in dehumanizing and objectifying women, yet which is construed as lovingly paternal:

> You'll let this man you love protect you and take care of you, is that it? You want this gold and shining powerful warrior to build a fortress for you to hide in so that you don't ever have to be afraid, or you don't

have to feel lonely, or you never have to feel empty—that's what you want, isn't it? . . . Well then it won't be long until he'll want you to build a fortress for him out of your tits and out of your cunt and out of your hair and your smile and the way you smell, someplace where he can feel comfortable enough and secure enough so that he can worship in front of the altar of his own prick. You're alone. You're all alone and you won't be able to be free of that feeling of being alone until you look death right in the face. . . . Until you go right up into the ass of death, and find the womb of fear. And then, maybe.

From the rest of the film, we know that Paul's intuition is correct: Tom objectifies Jeanne. His greatest desire is to film her all day long, "in the morning when you wake up, in the evening when you fall asleep, when you smile for the first time." When Jeanne is angry or upset, Tom creates image frames around her face with his hands, imagining what her display of emotion would look like on film. When she complains that his scopophilia is "raping her mind," he responds by delivering angry blows. Still, Tom believes that he loves Jeanne, for in his eyes she is "better than Rita Hayworth, than Joan Crawford, than Kim Novak; better than Lauren Bacall . . . than Ava Gardner when she was in love with Mickey Rooney."

The ideology explored in *Last Tango* through the juxtaposition of Paul and Tom[14] suggests that in the prevailing culture women are essentially objects for *visual* scrutiny; to see a woman is to know her. Seeing is equated with knowing, with believing. "Pornography conflates femininity with femaleness, femaleness with female sexuality, and female sexuality with a particular part of the female anatomy."[15] This is the specific promise of pornography: that femininity can be understood, can be dealt with and treated, through the visual scrutiny of women.

Pornography vs. Obscenity: The Legal Distinction

Indeed, equating female humanity with female sexuality appears so commonplace in pornographic representation that it caused Mac-Kinnon and Dworkin to address this matter in their well-publicized drafting of antipornography ordinances.[16] MacKinnon is a lawyer and professor of law; Dworkin is an author. Both are well known and have published extensively on such issues as sexual harassment, the physical abuse of women, the politics of sexuality, feminism as political theory, and of course pornography. Dworkin has written a book on pornography from a feminist standpoint, aptly entitled *Pornography: Men Possessing Women.*

In 1983, these women jointly proposed civil rights legislation aimed at stemming the presence, production, and proliferation of pornography in our culture. Together they drafted several versions of an ordinance designed to empower a plaintiff in claiming that his or her civil rights had been violated by the production, display, sale, or distribution of pornography. This civil rights approach to the issue was genuinely new: as a legal issue, pornography has always fallen under the rubric of the First Amendment. Traditionally, then, the key issue has been whether or not given pornographic displays constitute *protected* speech, i.e., speech protected under the Bill of Rights. Currently, if such displays are deemed unworthy of government protection, they are labeled "obscene."

This brings us to the legal understanding of the issue central to this investigation. Technically, "obscenity" denotes unprotected speech. The criteria employed in determining whether speech is obscene, and thus unprotected, derive from a 1973 Supreme Court decision, *Miller vs. California.* This case, involving brochures sent through the mail, produced a three-pronged standard putatively clarifying what distinguishes obscene speech. The Court held that all three of the following criteria must exist in order for any expression to be deemed unprotected: (a) the average person, applying contemporary community standards, would find that the work, taken as a whole, appeals to the prurient interest; (b) the work depicts or describes, in a patently offensive way, sexual conduct specified by the statute; and (c) the work, taken as a whole, lacks serious literary, artistic, political, or scientific value. Together, these three criteria identify forms of speech over which government might exert restraint. Generally, then, child pornography and certain types of hard core are deemed prima facie obscene.

But clearly much pornography does not meet the three criteria listed. This means that it is not legally obscene, and as such constitutes protected speech. Thus MacKinnon and Dworkin's proposal that pornography be viewed as a civil rights, rather than a First Amendment, issue presented a different tactic. It no longer mattered whether the speech in question was protected, for the issue central to the ordinance was not whether the government can or should enforce restraint. Instead, this new approach sought to enable victims of pornography to claim that their civil rights had been violated under certain conditions. Defining these conditions forced the articulation of precisely why these women find this system of representation objectionable. In its various incarnations, then, the ordinance always contained a section designed to clarify precisely what constitutes "pornographic" imagery, and enumerated criteria to that effect. The Minneapolis version of the ordinance identified nine criteria. Its sixth criterion cited the act of fragmentation as something that might cause a form of speech to be labeled "pornographic." It read: "Women's body parts—including but not limited to vaginas, breasts, and buttocks—are exhibited, such that women are reduced to those parts."[17] Under the logic of the ordinance, then, a woman could argue that pornography was dehumanizing given its fragmenting tendency and metonymic assertions. She would then need to prove that this dehumanization produced by fragmentation violated her civil rights.

Not all pornographic representations issue the stated equation. Many feminists maintain that images of men and women together, hard-core imagery, and certainly lesbian and gay pornography frequently contain a less objectionable politics, one which does not equate humanity with sexuality and bodily part. Yet the pornographic vision of female humanity as simply immanent, one justifiably reified and hypostatized, seemingly endorses this equation, and is thus found objectionable. It suggests that women should be deprived of the transcendent male realm, the realm of philosophy, metaphysics, art, literature, and science. Women are supposedly more immanent than men, more body than mind.

Metonymy, Fragmentation, and Fear

It is thus clear why pornography's metonymic, reductionist tendency might be found objectionable. What is less clear is why this reduction occurs in the first place. What drives this urge to collapse the intangible aspects of a woman, of a person, onto the material, visible plane, to deny the former in favor of the latter? What lies behind this perhaps unavowed yet extremely prevalent tendency to reify women, to hypostatize their being?

Contempt might be an obvious answer: contempt for women, for their devalued social status, for their traditional relegation to the private sphere, or, more so, for their recent inroads into the public. As we have seen, this empirical analysis underwrites the radical feminist position that views pornography in terms of social power relations—the cultural archeplot of gender hierarchy. I find this response convincing, yet taken alone it ultimately proves unsatisfactory. As suggested earlier, I believe there is more to male contempt for women than issues of *empirical* power. Misogyny is as much a psychoanalytic issue as it is a social and cultural one; our society breeds contempt for women based on not only who women are but on what they represent.

This investigation into obscenity relies on the claim that behind our culture's contempt for women lies fear—fear of otherness in general, and fear of the metaphorical and literal feminine in particular. This argument is not new; many have written of the ability of marginalized groups—women, African-Americans, Hispanics, Jews, lesbians, and gays—to threaten the dominant ideology and of the correlation between the threat they represent and the marginalization they subsequently experience. Marginalized groups become stereotyped and hated because of the disquiet they unleash in the hegemonic ruler, a disquiet forcing the dominant group to confront its own fallibility and to realize the tenuousness and relativity of its privilege. In Western culture, we value reason, progress, science, and technology; we posit the world as essentially knowable through empirical observation and study; we understand our relation to the natural world as one of justified domination, lording over the earth that we believe persists thanks to our intelligence, creativity, and agency. By virtue of our reason progress is forged, history is made.

Our constructions of otherness subsequently manifest qualities that counter this Cartesian prototype, qualities that—because they threaten those in power—are exaggerated, distorted, and even mendacious. The other is cast as bizarre, irrational, lazy, ignorant, overly emotional, greedy, sexually insatiable, mired in a strange, antiquated tradition. The other represents the obverse of all that the humanist tradition reveres; for some, this justifies the bigotry and contempt registered against it. Yet bigotry always bespeaks fear—fear of other possibilities, other sensibilities, other cognitive experiences of the world. The dominant group realizes this fact but denies it by projecting onto the other an exaggerated, stereotyped rendition of these possibilities. It constructs the other as more immanent than transcendent, more corporeal and materialist than intellectual and spiritual. The other appears threatening inasmuch as it seemingly fails to uphold the Western tradition of Enlightenment rationality and secular humanism. Susan Griffin writes:

The black man as stupid, as passive, as bestial; the woman as highly emotional, unthinking, a being closer to the earth. The Jews as a dark, avaricious race. . . . The usurious Jew. The African, a "greedy eater," lecherous, addicted to uncleanness. . . . The famous materialism of the Jew, the black, the woman. The woman who spends her husband's paycheques on hats. The black who drives a Cadillac while his children starve. The Jewish moneylender who sells his daughter. . . . The appetite which swallows. The black man who takes away a white man's job or the woman who takes a man's job. . . . The other has a body.[18]

Yet Griffin insists that the other is just as transcendent, intellectual, and spiritual as those in power; the other is maligned simply because its display of difference—be it sexual, racial, ethnic, or other—poses a threat. Edward Said's analysis of the Western construction of Orientals provides another example of such distorted images and projected fears.[19] Whereas the occidental world has traditionally maintained that Easterners owe us gratitude, the author insists that these groups have justified anger vis-à-vis the West given our imperialism, exploitation, and smugly patronizing attitude. In *Orientalism*, Said deplores the Western conviction that

Orientals or Arabs are . . . shown to be gullible, "devoid of energy and initiative," much given to "fulsome flattery," intrigue, cunning, and unkindness to animals; Orientals cannot walk on either a road or a pavement (their disordered minds fail to understand what the clever European grasps immediately, that roads and pavements are made for walking); Orientals are inveterate liars, they are "lethargic and suspicious," and in everything oppose the clarity, directness, and nobility of the Anglo-Saxon race.[20]

Paul Scott's *Jewel in the Crown* and E. M. Forster's *A Passage to India* both illustrate Said's point. These novels describe the erotic longings of British women for Indian men, longings that result in scandal. In both cases, the imperialist British establishment in India refuses to believe that the women are at all responsible for the troubling events. Instead, the scandals are explained solely in terms of the brutish, rapacious sexuality of Indian men who prey upon innocent British women. In Scott's novel, the Indian in question consequently suffers unjust torture and imprisonment. Hence Said's question: "Can one divide human reality . . . into clearly different cultures, histories, traditions, societies, even races, and survive the consequences humanly?"[21]

Memento Mori: Pornography as Containment

Let us now consider this exposition on otherness strictly in terms of women, and of pornography's objectification and fragmentation of the female body. We must ask what specifically the feminine reflects back to the masculine. What is so frightening there that it must be checked? What is so disturbing that, as Virginia Woolf writes, "[w]omen have served all these centuries as looking-glasses possessing the magic and delicious power of reflecting the figure of man at twice its natural size"?[22] The feminine is disturbing, I argue, because it reflects human mortality. It represents sensual immediacy, life as matter, the pleasurable but finite aspect of human existence. The feminine announces our vulnerability and ultimate lack of control. Standing in for the immanence in which we all partake, its message is *memento mori:* "you too shall die." I thus agree with the analyses of Griffin, Simone de Beauvoir,[23] Dorothy Dinnerstein,[24] and others that in our culture the feminine is permeated with death. Woman reflects back to man his own mortality, his finite existence, his immanence. For reasons that will be analyzed in the next chapter, a woman's body stands in for all that is aligned with nature, all that thwarts masculine cultural achievement; in sum, woman represents the pleasure principle as distinct from the reality principle. Equated with the body and hence sexuality, a woman "brings a man back" to his sensuous, material self, to that aspect of his existence that no amount of knowledge, information, or control can influence. In illustrating this point, de Beauvoir writes that "what a man cherishes and detests first of all in woman—loved one or mother—is the fixed image of his animal destiny; it is the life that is necessary to his existence but that condemns him to the finite and to death."[25]

In keeping with Western ideology, then, a woman defies the pretenses of secular humanism in its epistemological claims to power and control. Metaphorically, the feminine represents a foil to cultural achievement, to our investment in progress. It invokes a loss of identity, the death of the self. "From the day of his birth man begins to die: this is the truth incarnated in the Mother."[26] Griffin further argues that many people, especially men, are therefore threatened by sexuality inasmuch as it is aligned with a loss of control and of the self. Deep down, such persons actually find titillation humiliating:

Culture imagines itself to be invulnerable to nature. A man who believes culture's illusions believes that he is invulnerable to nature and that he controls nature. But the sight of a woman's body reminds him of the power of his own body, which is nature, over his mind, which is culture. Thus, for a few moments, his self-image dies and he is *humiliated.* . . . In one who is afraid of feeling . . . sexuality in itself constitutes a terrible threat.[27]

The metaphorical feminine capable of invoking this form of death thus runs counter to the theoretical tenets of secular humanism, our prevailing ideology. It represents a threat, an immanent and pleasurable realm that could swallow up masculine achievement, an engulfing abyss back into which his cultural acclimation could slide. In Dinnerstein's words: "The treacherous mermaid, seductive and impenetrable female representative of the dark and magic underwater world from which our life comes and in which we cannot live, lures voyagers to their doom."[28] This humiliation produced by female sexuality explains our culture's need to objectify and fragment the female body. Objectification and fragmentation work to deny female subjectivity, and this denial seeks to mitigate the threat of physical and psychic death that the feminine represents. For if a woman is truly reducible to bodily parts, how can she pose a threat? How can masculine achievement feel genuinely threatened by a leg, a hip, a breast?

Seen in this light, pornography's reification of female humanity bespeaks a self-protective displacement paralleling Freudian fetishism, discussed presently. It represents a form of wish fulfillment: would that women could not challenge the reality principle, could not represent immanence, the body, death, the other side of culture. Would that one could simply deny the threat that in fact motivates voyeurism. Simply put, pornography is a form of *containment.* It is this feminist reading of the genre which I find most compelling, one grounded in the radical feminist position but enriched by an understanding of masculine vulnerability. It is this reading that I rely upon in these pages. Pornography seeks to contain the female threat; it seeks to prevent her otherness from being put into play. Kuhn states this powerfully:

[C]ertain kinds of pornography may combine pleasure and unease— perhaps even at moments threatening to disrupt, rather than confirm, the spectator's masculinity. . . . Curiosity turns to terror, investigation to torture, the final affirmation of the objecthood of the other. The feminine here represents a threat to the masculine, a threat which demands containment.[29]

Hence while the radical feminist critique of pornography correctly focuses upon empirical power, domination, and privilege, it demands a fuller investigation of all that "the feminine" evokes— namely, death, the pleasure principle, and the dialectic between being and nonbeing. In the following chapters, I hope to demonstrate how the feminine recalls our combined fear and longing for psychic death, for the beyond, for the transgression of consensual limits. I hope to clarify how the feminine highlights the reality principle's vulnerability and mutability, and—by insisting upon the fluid, poetic nature of reality—how it invokes male hysteria. For in that it challenges the limits of culture and invokes a loss of control, a retreat from boundaries, a falling away from the self, the feminine is "obscene." In a culture steeped in the legacy of secular humanism, it demands containment.

One might conclude, then, that typically pornography's mission is to contain the obscene feminine, to hold its threat in check and disallow its primal quality to emerge. Scrutinized from this vantage point, much pornography appears objectionable because it is insufficiently obscene. It diverts us from the deepest insights into the dialectic between being and nonbeing that sexuality can provide, and thereby prohibits our apprehension of reality's fictitious nature. It denies the conflicted nature of human sexuality, striving to submit the latter to *logos* rather than be enmeshed in life and death impulses. Thus lacking the negativity that characterizes the obscene, pornography offers us an impoverished, undialectical version of human sexuality. In Kovel's words: "pornography . . . is the erotic less its negativity, less its ambivalence, its association of sexuality with death, and, finally, its truthfulness."[30]

Such insights demand further investigation, one enriched by a fuller psychoanalytic reading of the dangerous feminine, what Freud terms woman's "enemy" status.

CHAPTER TWO

The Contrapuntal Feminine and Male Hysteria

We have seen that the radical feminist critique of pornography interprets the male gaze largely in terms of men's power and authority over women. A competing feminist argument, one not incompatible with the radical position, instead understands the gaze in terms of male vulnerability. This position maintains that the gaze seeks to control women, yes, but only because the feminine threatens masculine hegemony by highlighting the tenuousness of its claims. Synthesizing these two positions—positions exemplified respectively in the writings of MacKinnon and Kuhn—proves useful to our discussion on obscenity: it forces us to ponder what is so primal, so uncanny in the feminine. What qualities in female otherness appear so terrifying that they demand the distanced containment that pornography provides?

In these pages, I expound upon the claim that the feminine is uncanny thanks to its contrapuntal status vis-à-vis the reality principle. Specifically, I use psychoanalysis to buttress the argument that woman recalls psychic death, the dialectic between being and nonbeing, the refusal to submit to *logos*. Bringing psychoanalytic tools to bear upon this analysis of the deathrattle contained in "the feminine," I examine this deathrattle, unmasking why it is precisely the feminine that causes us to go "right up into the ass of death," to "find the womb of fear." Such an analysis will further illustrate how certain feminist critiques of pornography encapsulate what is given play in the obscene.

Freud and the Centrality of Repression

There are numerous and varied schools of psychoanalytic thought. Those that arrive at the concept of a "dangerous feminine" do so via different routes. Here, we focus upon certain Freudian precepts that contribute to this notion; we also draw upon specific parallels between Freudian analysis, object relations theory, and Lacanian psychoanalysis, never drifting far from the pioneering inroads made by Freud. Together these schools of thought offer useful insights into the cultural construction of female otherness prevalent in the West, a construction closely linked to the obscene.

Freud's original contributions to the field of psychoanalysis build upon key premises; included among these are drive theory and repression. Freud posits two essential human drives: eros, the sexual drive, and thanatos, the death drive. For now, I would like to treat the concepts of repression and the erotic drive.

Freud views the achievements of civilization as founded upon repression.[1] He insists upon a struggle between the individual's basic, pleasure-seeking bodily impulses and the social need to repress those impulses. Culture cannot sustain itself, he argues, unless a restraining, taboo-ridden lexicon disallows or discourages some of the body's natural inclinations. The polymorphous perversion that characterized infancy—a perversion that knew no guilt, no restraint, in sum, no repression—must yield to culture's reality principle, for pleasure and sexuality operate against the interests of civilization. Thus according to Freud, human beings must internalize repression; otherwise pleasure would take over, so to speak, and we would never cooperate with civilization's mandates. Culture's commitment to the performance principle therefore presupposes taboo, all of which renders civilization "discontent." He writes:

> As we see, what decides the purpose of life is simply the programme of the pleasure principle. This principle dominates the operation of the mental apparatus from the start. There can be no doubt about its efficacy, and yet its programme is at loggerheads with the whole world, with the macrocosm as much as with the microcosm. There is no possibility at all of its being carried through; all the regulations of the universe run counter to it. One feels inclined to say that the intention that man should be "happy" is not included in the plan of "Creation." What we call happiness in the strictest sense comes from the (preferably sudden) satisfaction of needs which have been dammed up to a high degree. . . .[2]

This belief in a complicated cultural matrix organized around repression extends to the adult male and female bodies. As adults, we are enmeshed in taboo, for this matrix regionalizes, hierarchizes, and assigns our bodies meaning and value. Certain things have become private, guilt-ridden, illicit; we have internalized the reality principle that incorporates this matrix and insists on cultural laws, norms, and prohibitions. Interpreting what this matrix is and the values it assigns has of course provided ample fodder for various feminist criticisms of Freud, for this lexicon may be read as wrongly favoring the masculine norm over the putatively "deviant" female other.[3] Rather than reopen the long-standing debate between feminism and psychoanalysis, however, I wish to illustrate the usefulness of certain Freudian premises to our investigation. Specifically, I wish to suggest that even in Freud's own writings, female sexual difference is not codified singularly as deficiency, lack, or deviance. Rather it is a powerful contrapuntal force that can engulf, swallow up, and annihilate masculine cultural achievement.[4] In that the womb and vulva are construed as so primal, so defiant of acculturation, so countervailing against the reality principle, on one level they are more powerful than the penis. In a direct manner, this exploration of female "deviance" will inform our analysis of obscenity.

Freud claims that our polymorphous perverse impulses of infancy, that stage oblivious to the reality principle, yield to culture's norms once repression has been internalized; this internalization of course happens when we confront taboo forcefully during the oedipal phase. This phase—which presupposes a bourgeois family structure and the female care of young children—signals the child's heightened awareness and interpretation of the paternal presence, a presence that announces the impending breakup of the close relationship between mother and child, and the subsequent acclimation of the child to culture. Father is thus the envoy of culture, law, and order; his intervention invokes the child's renunciation of its perceived unilateral claim over mother, and inaugurates the child's acclimation to culture.

The bond between mother and child has preceded all social encounters; indeed, it comes before the child's recognition of society at all. With mother, the child knows an immediate world which has only gradually and incompletely been mediated. In the earliest phases of life, the child's perception of the world makes no distinction between mother and child, self and other; at the outset, no fundamental recognition of human subjectivity and objectivity prevails.[5]

The child has only a vague cognitive awareness of the world around it; there is no appreciation of culture's laws and dictates, nor of those fundamental pillars upon which civilization rests. While still in a pre-oedipal stage under the sway of the pleasure principle, the child's relationship to the world is only gradually becoming mediated by language and meaning. It is well known that this phase corresponds to Lacan's Imaginary, a concept of great importance to what is loosely and problematically termed "French feminism."[6] The pre-oedipal is also of special interest to object relations theorists, whose work of course has been amply employed by feminist scholars such as Nancy Chodorow, Carol Gilligan, Dorothy Dinnerstein, and Jessica Benjamin.[7]

The child's oblivion to culture prior to father's intervention led to Freud's description of the pre-oedipal phase as one of "oceanic oneness." This oneness, or sense of connection, owes itself to the child's originally unclear ego boundaries and a continued sense of attachment to the world. In the pre-oedipal stage dominated by mother, there is no clear sense of discrete self. The boundaries between "me" and "you" remain unfixed; everything is fluid. Admitting that he himself retained no memory of this feeling,[8] Freud nevertheless respected others' claims to such a memory and offered it theoretical support. For instance, he wrote of how a friend described this "oceanic" feeling as inspiring religious and mystical experience:

> Our present ego-feeling is . . . only a shrunken residue of a much more inclusive—indeed, an all-embracing—feeling which corresponded to a more intimate bond between the ego and the world about it. If we may assume that there are many people in whose mental life this primary ego-feeling has persisted to a greater or less degree, it would exist in them side by side with the narrower and more sharply demarcated ego-feeling of maturity, like a kind of counterpart to it. In that case, the ideational contents appropriate to it would be precisely those of limitlessness and of a bond with the universe—the same ideas with which my friend elucidated the "oceanic" feeling.[9]

This concept of a diffused oceanic pre-oedipal is similarly upheld by both Lacanian psychoanalysis and object relations theory. Lacan's adherence to this notion of a fluid pre-oedipal is what allowed him to pun on the word *l'hommelet*. During the pre-oedipal, Lacan argued, the "little man" has no firm sense of self as distinct from others; because his ego boundaries are completely permeable, he feels like an omelette. Hence feminist theorists employing Lacanian premises have scrutinized closely the fluid, irresolute, "maternal" qualities of the pre-oedipal, its profound impact on the human psyche, and inherently deconstructive attributes. Similarly, feminists employing object relations theory have analyzed the primary bond that prevails between mother and child during the fluid pre-oedipal. This bond has a powerful impact on the child's development and psychology, they argue; the specific development of girls, however, remains insufficiently understood within the framework of traditional paradigms. Their analyses have led them to endorse altered family structures, insisting that in order for certain human psychopathologies to change, the pre-oedipal must be imbued with both a female and male presence.

Certainly problems inhere whenever one posits an absolute theoretical foundation such as this. Indeed, I am fully aware of the dangers implicit in endorsing the maternal's role as a utopian point of origin.[10] I simply wish to emphasize the importance given to the maternal body, and to its initial loss, by several schools of psychoanalytic thought. This loss figures prominently in my understanding of how, in our culture, the feminine is cast as contrapuntal.

Let me return, then, to Freud's insights. His analysis highlights culture's mandate that the pre-oedipal childhood bond with mother be delimited, that the child abandon the physical, emotional closeness experienced with her in favor of culture's mandates. This cultural prohibition on sexual relations among family members is the incest taboo. It corresponds to the exogamy dictum that Freud identified as so fundamental to civilization. This taboo gradually attenuates the union between mother and child; unlike father, the child has no sexual claim over mother. Of course, relinquishing mother to father's marital claims creates conflict in the child. In seeking a solution to the conflict, however, the child may not simply annihilate the father: This emanates from the cultural prohibition surrounding murder. There is no choice, then, but for the child to accept the culturally sanctioned bond between its parents; father's hold over mother is unhampered while the child itself loses ground. Hence in disrupting the mother-child dyad, the "oedipal" phase forces the child to recognize the paternal presence and to internalize cultural laws and norms.

As stated earlier, this disruption occurs thanks to the child's awakening to the meaning with which father's presence and authority are imbued. Father signifies the fact that the child's claim over the mother is limited, that their union must be mediated by the surrounding culture. He designates that "maternal" oceanic oneness and the pleasure principle must yield to an individuated identity be-holden to the reality principle. In contrast to mother's nurturance, her apparent grounding in nature and association with the pleasure principle, then, father evokes cultural laws, prohibitions, and taboos; along with these come the performance principle, progress, and human achievement. Father stands in for the necessary cultural con-ditioning that upholds civilization, especially as concerns the body. He dictates that immediate sensual gratifications and impulses must be harnessed in order for human culture to proceed. The oedipal stage thus describes that time when the child fully internalizes the dichotomy between an immediate, impulsive, "maternal" world and one which is structured, taboo-ridden, achievement-oriented, and "phallic." Both object relations theory and Lacanian thought simi-larly recognize this dichotomy in gender archetypes: for both schools, the pre-oedipal is "maternal," unmediated by culture's mandates and taboos; conversely, the oedipal is "paternal" or "phallic," behold-ened to culture's laws, prohibitions, conventions, and the performance principle.

As stated, this internalization of culture's taboos extends to the human body and "organizes" it definitively. Central to the child's acclimation to culture stands his or her recognition of the fact that bodily impulses demand restraint: polymorphous perversion must be harnessed and controlled in favor of a socially acceptable, work-oriented, procreative body. Issues of human sexuality, scatology, and general hygiene now assume a private status and become charged with moral overtones; the child recognizes that a "genitally orga-nized" body—one that, in keeping with the Victorian ethos of Freud's time, finds its sexual expression through genital contact with a member of the opposite sex—alone is culturally sanctioned and should thus supplant the many types of bodily gratification that the child formerly enjoyed. The human body becomes regionalized, with certain parts of it bound up with shame and disgust. Indeed, the paternal injunction to embrace culture's norms proves so powerful as to produce disdain and contempt in the child for bodily attributes and processes about which he or she formerly had no opinion.

Perseus, Medusa, and Male Hysteria

Classical psychoanalysis couples this oedipal phase with the male child's beholding the nude female body. This is a horrifying experience inasmuch as the sight of a nude woman instills in him anxiety regarding the potential loss of his masculine organ. The woman appears to be castrated, maimed, "decapitated." The sight of her is at once fascinating and terrifying: fascinating for the sexual feelings her body awakens in the boy, terrifying for the threat that this sight of sexual difference poses to the supposedly hegemonic masculine libidinal economy. In "Medusa's Head," Freud writes:

> To decapitate = to castrate. The terror of (the female genitals) is thus a terror of castration that is linked to the sight of something. Numerous analyses have made us familiar with the occasion for this: it occurs when a boy, who has hitherto been unwilling to believe the threat of castration, catches sight of the female genitals. . . .[11]

The penis—hallmark of the reality principle, father's authority, and the power of reason—now stands threatened, its hegemonic, orderly rule menaced by an inchoate, diffused feminine realm, psychically still linked to the pleasure principle. Indeed, this sight of bodily difference throws open a number of questions about the masculine and feminine realms that the child has hitherto been assessing. How does he internalize his perceptions that the parent associated with authority and cultural prohibition still claims a penis, whereas mother—associated with polymorphous perversion, oceanic oneness, and the absence of cultural laws—has seemingly lost hers? He internalizes this as a mandate to further cling to the dictates of culture, lest he himself be castrated. Honoring the paternal role through further acclamation to culture thus appears as a means of safeguarding the masculine self against the female plight. The more one upholds culture's dictates, the boy reasons, the more one protects against castration. Hence the sight of the female genitals instills both desire and anxiety in the boy, inspiring his own increased identification with paternal authority that alone can keep this threat at bay. This is castration anxiety which—given its investment in male authority, privilege, and control—provides the underpinnings of male hysteria.

Freud concedes that this reading of the female body is pervasive among men, at least in Western culture: "[p]robably no male human being is spared the fright of castration at the sight of the female genital."[12] He expounds on how powerfully female difference threatens the masculine point of reference by frequently drawing on myth. For instance, as intimated earlier, he writes of Medusa, one of three terrifying mythical monsters known as Gorgons, whose hair consists of "a mass of twisting snakes."[13] So frightening are these three monsters that, when looked upon, they turn their viewers to stone:

> And they are three, the Gorgons, each with wings
> And snaky hair, most horrible to mortals.
> Whom no man shall behold and draw again
> The breath of life[.][14]

According to myth, Perseus, son of Zeus and Danae, becomes eager to decapitate Medusa in order to offer her head as a gift to the bride of Polydectes. How might he accomplish this task, thereby annihilating her threat, without himself turning to stone? Only by using five accoutrements, given to him as gifts: a mirroring shield, an unbreakable, unbending sword, winged shoes, a magic wallet, and a hat that makes its wearer invisible. When outfitted with these gifts—which protect, shield, buffer, and divert the direct impact of Medusa on Perseus—he can attack the horrifying monster. The myth recounts the triumph of Perseus. Cellini's famous bronze statue thus reveals a victorious Perseus holding the severed head of Medusa.

This terrifying Medusa head, covered with twisting snakes, is obviously likened to the female genitals. The head's ability to turn its viewer to stone resonates with the combined arousal and terror that female otherness instills in the masculine heart. It suggests that the sight of female sexual difference is simultaneously exciting and disempowering; the male viewer is at once titillated and threatened by the sight of the female genitals, and both responses "turn him to stone." Hence the male stiffening constitutes an overdetermined response, one having various causes:

> The sight of Medusa's head makes the spectator stiff with terror, turns him to stone. Observe that we have here once again the same origin from the castration complex and the same transformation of affect! For becoming stiff means an erection. Thus in the original situation it offers consolation to the spectator: he is still in possession of a penis, and the stiffening reassures him of the fact.[15]

Of these two responses, arousal and anxiety, I wish to first concentrate on the latter.

Perseus with head of Medusa, Benvenuto Cellini (1500–1571), Loggia de'Lanzi, Florence, Italy. Photograph courtesy Alinari/Art Resources, New York.

So great is the terror that Medusa strikes in her antagonist's heart that she cannot be confronted directly. Were Perseus "turned to stone" (overwhelmed by female difference, threatened by sexuality, returned to his body), he would be unable to wield his unbreakable, unbending "sword." So great is the anxiety that the sight of her produces that the abundant snakes covering her head may in fact be read as substitute male organs: according to Freud, their substitution serves to mitigate the overwhelming terror delivered by female otherness. He explains: "It is a remarkable fact that, however frightening (the snakes) may be in themselves, they nevertheless serve actually as a mitigation of the horror, for they replace the penis, the absence of which is the cause of the horror."[16] It follows, then, that the head's decapitation represents actual castration, a fate in store for the boy who fails to abide by culture's dictates.

Male castration anxiety is central to Freud's theory of masculine psychosexual development; it also provides the background needed to explain other aspects of his theory. For instance, it buttresses the claim that fetishism represents a male obsession. Fetishism seeks to counter castration anxiety by drawing attention toward some other aspect of the body—say, a foot—or toward some object, in an effort to detract from the genitals. It is a defense mechanism seeking to appease the terror that female sexual difference can produce. It bespeaks castration anxiety, and the hysteria that accompanies the inability to accept the penis as but one cultural signifier among many.

Important to our analysis is the fact that castration anxiety and the fear of female difference also underwrite the claim that women are putatively the "enemies of civilization." For if, motivated by castration anxiety, a little boy internalizes paternal authority more than a girl, it follows that he will identify especially with the "paternal" realm: civilization, culture, law, prohibition—in sum, the super-ego. Conversely, Freud claims that girls internalize paternal authority less avidly; they "come into opposition to civilization and display their retarding and restraining influence. . . ."[17] It is this "uncivilized" enemy status, what Sarah Kofman calls woman's "criminal" element, which buttresses my assertions about the dangerous feminine, ultimately forging a link between the female body and the category of the obscene. The female genitals are the envoys of otherness; they denote the other side of civilization. They challenge the limits of culture, calling into question our internalized repression and invoking a sense of psychic death. Hence according to classical psychoanalytic theory, nothing in our culture so challenges the reality principle as the female body, the Medusa-like genitals. Indeed, Freud writes that "in Rabelais . . . the Devil took flight when [a] woman showed him her vulva."[18]

Let me be clear, then, that "the feminine" represents more than an arrangement of specific bodily parts. Linked to the female genitals that invoke the dionysian realm of anti-organization, the metaphorical feminine denotes a defiance of the reality principle, the other side of civilization, a call to the outside of meaning. Because it resists the organizing influences of culture, remaining inchoate, "oceanic," and diffused, the feminine invokes a loss of self, challenges the limits of culture, and underscores the reality principle's tenuousness. For our investigation, this tenuousness invoked by the feminine is key. It is precisely what obscenity puts into play, be it with a rude gesture, a dirty word, a disturbing piece of graffiti, a shocking photograph. Like the feminine, obscenity recalls an un-mediated relationship between the body and the world, and a dedifferentiated relationship wherein union, fusion, and oneness prevail over separation, individuation, and autonomy. It stands as a reminder that below the surface of our distinct identities and acclimation to cultural mandates there exists a more primal sense of being, one approximating a state of psychic death and the experience of continuity. Indeed, it follows that the feminine is associated with the transgressive, continuous realm existing both prior to and beyond the conscious way in which we experience the world. Here, "prior" refers to the continuity characteristic of the pre-oedipal oceanic oneness; "beyond" to the continuity found in death, the transgression of boundaries, and the fusion between self and other which occurs in sex. Both refer to the continuous dimension wherein distinct ego boundaries fall away. Hence the rock group The Cutting Crew sings:

> I just died in your arms tonight
> It must have been something you said
> I just died in your arms tonight
> It must have been some kind of kiss
> I should have walked away

The dionysian feminine therefore invokes a loss of self, a loss of cultural matrix, the dissolution of civilization's fundamental precepts. It aligns itself not with a cognitive recognition of human mortality (for this is comprised in the reality principle) but with a form of psychic death that defies civilization's organizing principles (and thus resonates with the pleasure principle). In thus challenging the limits of culture, the feminine is obscene and gives rise to castration anxiety.

Fear of the Primal Mother

Freud's writings further elucidate the question of how the male and female bodies are culturally construed, with the masculine positioned as the envoy of culture, and the feminine its countervailing opponent.[19] Specifically, these writings suggest that castration anxiety arises not so much from the sight of female difference as from the perceived threat of being reabsorbed back into the maternal, reengulfed by the pleasure principle, polymorphous perversion, oceanic oneness, and the dedifferentiated existence that female otherness denotes. Because he has so much invested in culture's mandates, in individual agency and autonomy, the boy fears reabsorption by the mother, under whose auspices his identity will founder.

Castration anxiety therefore refers not only to a boy's fear of paternal punishment and consequent emasculation; it also reveals his dread of women, whom he perceives as capable of leveling male endeavors, of swallowing him up and ruining the progress of civilization. "She can . . . readily re-evoke in him the unqualified, boundless, helpless passion of infancy," writes Dinnerstein; "[i]f he lets her, she can shatter his adult sense of power and control; she can bring out the soft, wild, naked baby in him."[20] Fear of reabsorption into the maternal thus exemplifies the subtlety of Freud's work, for his later writings theorize that children, especially boys, so fear reabsorption into the primal, terrifying, all-encompassing mother that, to a good extent, the oedipal phase is *self-imposed*. This reading of the oedipal has also been analyzed extensively by Janine Chasseguet-Smirgel.[21] The pre-oedipal, "phallic" mother proves too overwhelming, too primal for the child, who seeks shelter from her in the form of a protective, authoritative father located in the here and now of the reality principle. Thus it is not the father who actively intervenes between mother and child; rather, paternal intervention is wished for and sought out by the child to aid in the latter's attempts to delimit the seemingly boundless power of mother. "[T]he infant's helplessness and the longing for the father aroused by it seem to be incontrovertible," writes Freud. "I cannot think of any need in childhood as strong as the need for a father's protection."[22] Herbert Marcuse's *Eros and Civilization: A Philosophical Inquiry into Freud*, analyzed in more detail later, contains a passage supporting our observations about the powerful and frightening maternal:

> As the reality principle takes root, even in its most primitive and most brutally enforced form, the pleasure principle becomes something frightful and even terrifying; the impulses for free gratification meet with anxiety and this anxiety calls for protection against them. The individuals have to defend themselves against the specter of their integral liberation from want and pain, against integral gratification. And the latter is represented by the woman who, as mother, has once, for the first and last time, provided such gratification.[23]

Hence it is not only the law-imposing, punishing father who instills fear in the child—in her ability to swallow up and annihilate the child's burgeoning sense of self, the mother in fact appears more ominous. Hallmark of the pleasure principle, the archaic, primal mother threatens to undermine the reality principle, demonstrate its conceit, and unleash the dionysian impulses that in fact underlie its pretense to an organized body, a repressive social ethos, a civilization founded on taboo. It follows, then, that culture's efforts to contain the literal and metaphorical maternal, to delimit its power and undermine its abilities, emanate from a subconscious awareness of the power that the maternal wields. The feminine here is a threat that must be contained. Privileging the masculine over the feminine thus reveals itself as a political maneuver, not a given of nature.

This concept of a contrapuntal maternal, so integral to my reading of the obscene, is also given play by other scholars. For instance, the enterprise of psychically and empirically delimiting female power has been termed "beating back" the mother by feminists drawing upon object relations theory, particularly Jessica Benjamin.[24] Benjamin insists that "beating back" is an especially masculine undertaking, because masculinity defines itself more in terms of the reality principle than does female identity, which explains why men would be more afraid of the engulfing, annihilating feminine than women.

Operating within a Lacanian framework that similarly acknowledges the feminine's contrapuntal status, Julia Kristeva has also written extensively on the maternal's defiance of identity. Like other French feminist scholars—whose work remains nevertheless quite variegated—she understands the maternal as a foil to phallogocentrism's investment in the reality principle. Forever aligned with the pre-oedipal phase unmediated by culture, the maternal is an antidote to human identity and thus a metaphor for all that resists closure, remaining fluid, poetic, deliberately irresolute and deconstructive. In "Stabat Mater," for instance, she describes the maternal's dissipating influence:

> Trying to think through that abyss: staggering vertigo. No identity holds up. A mother's identity is maintained only through the well-known closure of consciousness within the indolence of habit, when a woman protects herself from the borderline that severs her body and expatriates it from her child. . . . [M]otherhood destines us to a demented *jouissance* that is answered, by chance, by the nursling's laughter in the sunny waters of the ocean. What connection is there between it and myself? No connection, except for that overflowing laughter where one senses the collapse of some ringing, subtle, fluid identity or other, softly buoyed by the waves.[25]

The Metaphorical Feminine, the Literal Female Body

This discussion on the primal mother is integral to my argument. It feeds directly into the feminist critique of the vulnerable gaze and forges a link between the pornography debates and the general topic of obscenity. What is this link? It is the conceptual resonance between the maternal or feminine and the obscene: both are aligned with the pleasure principle and provide continuity. Both defy discontinuity, run counter to culture's organization, and unravel human identity. The terrifying and exciting female genitals, the vulnerable male gaze, pornography as containment, "beating back" the mother, fetishism: These concepts demonstrate the combined fear and pleasure that the female body holds in its promise of continuity, and its attendant ability to challenge the limits of culture. In this, it is "obscene." Viewed in this light, pornography's obsession with the female genitals becomes a shorthand for what is always at play with the obscene: the need for continuity alloyed to fear of it; a desire to lose the self accompanied by dread of the same; a sense of the uncanny always present in our eagerness to visit the other side of civilization. The feminist critique of pornography that I have insisted upon here thus encapsulates what obscenity is about. It is precisely the feminine or maternal that takes us "into the ass of death," allowing us to find "the womb of fear."

We now understand more fully the metonymic, reductionist impulses of pornography in which "women's body parts . . . are exhibited, such that women are reduced to those parts." They express the need to contain female otherness, to disregard its deconstructive potential and its negative moment. Fetishism and fragmentation dramatize the wish fulfillment contained in pornography's effort to collapse female humanity onto isolated bodily parts. Would that the feminine were so utterly reifiable, so easily hypostatized. Then the meaning ascribed to the female genitals could be overlooked, and "the feminine" might refer to something easily contained rather than eminently deconstructive, forever eluding the grasp of *logos* and announcing the presence of the unconscious, the unknown, and the unmediated.

Timothy Beneke's interviews with rapists, discussed in his article "Intrusive Images and Subjectified Bodies: Notes on Visual Heterosexual Porn,"[26] corroborate these insights. In agreement with the contention that pornography frequently bespeaks male vulnerability, Beneke surmises "that sexual arousal loosens ego boundaries"; hence it follows that "the essence of porn is to seek arousal and gratification without vulnerability, without risk of the self."[27] Throughout the interviews, the rapists' painful confessions illustrate the degree to which the mere presence of a female body can be perceived as threatening, as an intrusion, an unwelcome disruption to their sense of self. One man explains:

> I have been injured by women. By the way they look, move, smell, and behave, they force me to have sexual sensation I didn't want to have. If a man rapes a sexy woman, he is forcing her to have sexual sensation she doesn't want to have. It is just revenge.[28]

Others concede:

> Growing up, I definitely felt teased by women. . . . I definitely felt played with, used, manipulated, like women were testing their power over me. I hated it with a passion! With a *fucking* passion!

> When you see a girl walking around wearing real skimpy clothes, she's offending you.

> Where I work it's probably no different from any other major city in the U.S. The women dress up in high heels and they wear a lot of

makeup, and they just look really hot and really sexy and how can somebody who has a healthy sex drive not feel lust for them?

I feel that (women) have power over men just by their presence. Just the fact that they can come up to me and just melt me and make me feel like a dummy makes me want revenge.[29]

I find the term "melt" revealing when posited as an inciter to revenge, for it resonates with the claim that the feminine loosens ego boundaries and puts us in touch with those disturbing, threatening aspects of sexual desire. Stated more broadly, it corroborates the claim that female sexual difference metaphorically invokes the other side of our organized identities, challenges the limits of culture, and puts us in touch with something primal and uncanny.

The Obscene: Not Only
Sexual, Not Only Disturbing

Indeed, our encounters with the obscene feminine, the other side of civilization, are not always pleasurable. Nor are they only sexual. Although this investigation isolates the topic of pornography, I wish to emphasize that the obscene comprises many things that defy the reality principle and challenge the limits of culture. These things usually center around the human body but are not only sexual. For instance, the book *The Three Faces of Eve* recounts the true story of a mentally ill woman with several personalities. Distraught, she seeks help through psychotherapy. With the aid of her doctor she gradually uncovers a painful memory that provides some insight into her problem: As a young child, she was forced to kiss the corpse of a deceased family member laid out in a casket. In my reading of things, such an act is potentially "obscene." Kissing a dead body ran counter to internalized repression and sufficiently challenged the limits of culture to traumatize a young girl. Hence later in life this stored-away trauma contributed to her mental illness.

Yet I insist that the obscene, contrapuntal, "enemy" status of women awakens more than hostile feelings, for it represents more than a threatening force in need of containment. I would argue that the feminine—and indeed many things relating to the body or to death—concatenate an invariable admixture of horror and pleasure, dread and desire; we long for dedifferentiation, continuity, and psychic death as much as we fear it. There is no singularity in the responses drawn from the obscene. In *The Prince*, Machiavelli writes with conviction that the ruthless Cesare Borgia, ruler of an Italian city, did well to place a corpse rent in two in the public square, a bloody knife and piece of wood beside it. "The ferocity of this scene left the people at once stunned and satisfied."[30]

The fact that transgressing boundaries, losing the self, and defying the reality principle can indeed be pleasurable explains why our culture needs the category of the obscene. Let us delve deeper into this impulse not to contain the obscene but to experience it. For only when we fully grasp what is experienced in obscenity can we appreciate why this topic is so powerful, so emotionally charged, so essential to human culture. Only when we acknowledge how the ideas discussed here play themselves out in response to human desire can we fully grasp why the feminine, the other, needs to remain obscene.

CHAPTER THREE

Thanatos, Abjection, and the "Race Toward Death"

In keeping with psychoanalytic theory, the sight of the unclothed female body evokes an admixture of fear and desire in the viewer, especially the male viewer. It is especially the female genitals that recall dedifferentiation, continuity, and a sense of reality unaligned with culture's laws, prohibitions, and taboos; as envoys of otherness, they combine pleasure with unease, never settling into a single system of meaning. Like Medusa, they are monstrous Gorgons. One wishes to possess them yet dreads contemplating them directly lest one "turn to stone" (be annihilated, swallowed by the mother, returned to dedifferentiation). The feminist critique of pornography that interprets this system of representation as seeking to contain even as it enjoys the sight of the female genitals therefore encapsulates what is given play in the obscene: the dialectic between being and nonbeing. We have examined the fear and horror produced by the sight of female difference; here, we explore the desire it inspires.

By desire, I refer not merely to sexual arousal. I also refer to the specific longing for reabsorption back into the maternal-as-metaphor, back into a continuous, dedifferentiated existence unscathed by the reality principle, devoid of internalized repression, untouched by civilization's organizing influence over human experience and the human body. A woman's body stands in for a subversive system of meaning in contrast to the ordered, paternal realm of the reality principle; it displays the possibility of assuming an oppositional disposition vis-à-vis the reality principle. Hence our desire for reabsorption back into the maternal represents a longing to transgress the boundaries of self, to experience a psychic death and be joined to the world in a way normally precluded by our everyday, individuated identities. We have seen that this dedifferentiated, self-annihilating aspect of the maternal constitutes the link between it and the category of the obscene. Both refer to continuity, to the terrifying and pleasurable realm of non-individuation that—inasmuch as it transgresses our habitual, discrete boundaries of self—exists as heir to the religious tradition.

Rather than simply wanting to beat back the maternal's oppositional system of meaning, then, we also desire reabsorption into it. This desire reveals our longing to be re-engulfed and overwhelmed by its contrapuntal significance, joined to the continuity it evokes. Why this desire to be reabsorbed, to challenge the limits of culture?

In answering this question, we return to drive theory. We recall that, for Freud, certain innate impulses reside in every human being, impulses that—quite separate from given experiences—are ingrained at the very level of instinct and energy flow. It is this adherence to drive theory that precludes the statement that our desire for reabsorption and continuity emanates simply from our experience of pre-oedipal dedifferentiation, from our memories as an inchoate, diffused self. Indeed, I believe that this desire for reabsorption back into the maternal grounds itself in something more than the *memory* of dedifferentiation; surely Freud is not alone in having no recollection whatsoever of the "oceanic oneness" characterizing this period. More to the point, the claims of memory pale beside the more forceful assertions promulgated by drive theory. Thusfar, we have discussed the erotic drive in terms of human sexuality, taboo, and cultural protocol. Yet I believe that thanatos, the death drive, plays at least as great a role in a discussion of obscenity as does eros. Specifically, thanatos explains more fully our deep need for the obscene in terms of the latter's promise of continuity. It thus explains why this category is so integral to culture.

Thanatos: Our Impulse
Toward Dedifferentiation

Drive theory draws on Freud's early training as a neuropathologist. This helps explain why for him eros and thanatos represent basic impulses or instincts innate to the human organism. Importantly, the two remain forever alloyed. In *Civilization and Its Discontents*, Freud specifically describes the erotic drive as an impulse toward preservation of the living self, an impulse that leads the individual to be joined with other, larger units. Eros desires other human beings; it contains an energetic, creative impulse. Seeking pleasure and a release of tension, it must be harnessed by civilization in order to serve the latter's purposes. It is forward-looking, and strives toward a state of things not yet attained. However, in *Beyond the Pleasure Principle*, Freud contrasts this life-affirming drive with its obverse, which is conservative, retrograde, and seeks to recreate the past and ultimately dispel the organism's energy. Thanatos, the death drive, dissolves those elements joining the self to larger units in an effort to achieve a more primitive, archaic form of existence. This drive longs for homeostasis, a state devoid of energy. It is therefore a retrograde impulse having its origins in the inorganic stage of life. In this, it reveals how all living organisms evolved in specific ways yet retain in their very composition an inclination toward returning to that stage, toward dying in a highly specific manner suitable to that organism. Hence the death drive can actually prolong life by diverting the organism from deaths not appropriate to it. This drive represents a conservative impulse, the desire on the part of the organism to avoid increases in tension, to preserve what it has, and to keep things as close to a state of homeostasis as possible. Unlike eros, it eschews what is dynamic in favor of what is static. This is why Freud also referred to the death drive as the "Nirvana principle," the absence of tension, a state of continuity, homeostasis, and nonindividuation. Indeed, thanatos seeks nothing less than to dispel the tensions that inhere in our individuated existences.

This tendency toward homeostasis helps explain the death drive's "repetition compulsion," the urge to repeat the past in an effort to keep it intact, to allow the organism's life span to assume a trajectory commensurate with its species. This impulse acts to prevent the organism from going off in new directions, striving instead to keep it on a specific and familiar track. Thanatos seeks to countervail the erotic self,

> to ward off any possible ways of returning to inorganic existence other than those which are immanent in the organism itself. . . . What we are left with is the fact that the organism wishes to die only in its own fashion.[1]

Hence eros, "the true life instincts," moves forward with sexual energy and impulse; thanatos holds that impulse in check given
its retrograde tendency, its longing for an earlier state of things.
According to Freud, life must be understood in terms of these two
fundamental drives. Yet in *Beyond the Pleasure Principle*, he privileges the death drive over the erotic impulse by claiming that its
retrograde tendency emanates from the initial, primary state of human life. Hence Freud posits human life and human instincts as
fundamentally conservative:

> It would be in contradiction to the conservative nature of the instincts
> if the goal of life were a state of things which had never yet been
> attained. On the contrary, it must be an old state of things, an initial
> state from which the living entity has at one time or other departed
> and to which it is striving to return by the circuitous paths along
> which its development leads.[2]

If thanatos claims a primary status over eros, yet remains forever alloyed to it, it follows that sexual expression bears the imprint of these conservative impulses. This is a way of saying that
our erotic, discontinuous selves remain alloyed to our impulse toward continuity and dedifferentiation, toward recalling our status as
members of a species answering to the dictates of that species. I
thus identify the primary status of thanatos as a pivotal concept with
regard to obscenity, for the latter is fundamentally about our desire
for continuity, our eagerness to escape the "numbing encasement"[3]
of individuation.

We have seen that the feminine or maternal as constituted in
our culture resonates with the continuous realm prevailing prior to
the differentiation of the reality principle. It is this resonance that
renders the female body both arousing and disturbing, for the genitals recall this nonindividuated, contrapuntal state and helps assign
the feminine its "enemy" status. Hence those qualities with which
the maternal is imbued—the annihilation of self, psychic death, the
outside of meaning—stand commensurate with the death drive.

Thus I would argue that the pre-oedipal experience of nonindividuation—those moments truly unscathed by the reality principle,
in which we are Lacan's *hommelets*—approximates the instinct of
thanatos more closely than does our individuated, acclimated experiences of self. For instance, while insisting that "Freud notes that
the most instinctual drive is the death drive,"[4] Julia Kristeva writes

that the pre-oedipal "has only one quality of the object—that of being opposed to *I*. . . . It is no longer I who expel, 'I' is expelled."[5] And now we understand how passing from discontinuity to continuity—being reabsorbed back into the maternal—might be construed as responding to a primary *instinct*. This explains the enormous appeal of the female genitals, of the metaphorical feminine, and of obscenity in general. They all respond to our most basic drive. The feminine thus corresponds not only to a cognitive awareness of human mortality—*memento mori*—but resonates with thanatos, our instinctive desire to retreat from boundaries.

This exposition on the death drive completes our understanding of the maternal as something truly primal and archaic, truly in opposition to civilization, yet essential. It clarifies why, in our culture, obscenity represents such a needed and highly charged category, one enmeshed in the maternal. Indeed, our desire for the contrapuntal maternal explains the essential place that obscenity holds within our culture. Death, continuity, dedifferentiation, what Kristeva calls the "abject" or outside-of-meaning: These attributes of the obscene, which oppose it to the reality principle, assure its integral status in a culture so committed to progress, technology, and individual achievement while operating against the backdrop of the death drive. Obscenity answers our need to be able to renegotiate the reality principle, to know that a fuller, more poetic sense of the world exists against our individuated, highly organized perceptions of it. It gives expression to our primal yearning for self-annihilation, thus reminding us of the necessary dialectic between our discontinuous and continuous selves that brings to the fore an otherwise muted undercurrent of our existence.

The following passage from Joyce Rebeta-Burditt's *The Cracker Factory* illustrates this longing for continuity that seeks reabsorption into the maternal. Cassie and Cara are patients in a psychiatric ward, where "life . . . bears a certain resemblance to an ocean cruise."[6] Inside the ward, they ponder their experiences as women:

"Have you ever had a man tell you he would like to crawl up inside you and stay there?" Cara asked thoughtfully.

"Sure," I answered. "Stay there where it's safe is the way I've heard it put."

"Have you ever told a man that you would like to crawl up inside HIM?"

"And snuggle in his intestines. Hell, no. I've never for a minute thought it would be safe inside a man. . . ."

"No womb," Cara decided. "Most of the guys I know want to return
to the womb. And I'm supposed to feel flattered because it's my womb
they want to return to."

"Maybe Mommy won't have them. . . ."[7]

Given that the death drive is posited as universal, however, it
follows that both men and women experience such a longing for
reabsorption back into the maternal. Due to their heightened investment in the reality principle, however, perhaps men experience this
longing more acutely.

Inasmuch as it opposes and undermines the reality principle,
the obscene paradoxically brings us to life. Let me emphasize here
that thanatos resonates with the obscene not on an exclusively mor-
bid or sinister plane. Rather, I believe that it also resonates along
spiritual and aesthetic lines, for only when, in response to the death
drive, we annihilate our differentiated existences can we apprehend
the world's fullness. Giving play to this dialectic unleashes a spir-
itually heightened sense of the world, one that is not nameable and
ordered. It challenges the reality principle and reveals the fluid,
dionysian realm as truthful, more compelling because more primal.

In this, obscenity is heir to our religious tradition. Susan Sontag describes obscenity as "the voluptuous yearning for the extinc-
tion of one's consciousness, for death itself."[8] Others confirm this
connection between the urge for erotic expression and deathly annihilation, a connection that sustains the religious heritage of the
West. The Judeo-Christian tradition insists that self-denial and self-
sacrifice breed a fuller connection between the self, the world, and
God. "The whole business of eroticism is to destroy the self-contained character of the participators as they are in their normal
lives," George Bataille observes, concluding that, because it attenuates the distinction between self and other, "eroticism is primarily
a religious matter."[9] For example, Saint Francis of Assisi's "The
Canticle of the Sun" extols the virtues of humility and self-denial
while referring to the elements of nature in familial terms—brother
sun, wind, and fire; sister moon, stars, and water. Moreover, it is
well known that Saint Francis spoke and even preached to birds,
just as Saint Anthony of Padua did to fishes.

Indeed, the submissive self-effacing that is part and parcel of
the Judeo-Christian tradition parallels our culture's need for the
obscene. Obscenity illustrates our ability and desire to pass from
discontinuity to continuity, to experience the world on a dediffer-

entiated plane. Its mission is at once spiritual, psychic, and sexual. I wish to highlight the parallels between the primal, maternal realm of the obscene and the Western religious tradition, especially how an existence more attuned to the pleasure principle buttresses the belief in human redemption. There are striking parallels between the psychoanalytic enterprise and the redemption of the flesh, for both strive to make conscious the unconscious. For instance, a basic precept of Christianity lies in transcending everyday boundaries and acclaiming continuity. The notions of resurrection, communion, life everlasting, and the world's timelessness would remain implausible without the transgression of worldly boundaries and an unmediated relationship to meaning. With the elimination of boundaries, we are freed from an historical sense of time and can conceive of a "world without end." We can make sense of such statements as "the kingdom of God is within you" and accept the assertion that Jesus was concurrently human and divine. A retreat from boundaries and defiance of the reality principle thus allow for the regeneration of human flesh. Communion serves as an example. For believers, communion is not a symbol of Christ, it is Christ. When ordained ministers distribute this sacrament, they state plainly: "This is the body of Christ." Hence sacred and profane join hands, for religion, like obscenity, proves a foil to the reality principle. The regenerated flesh casts off the traces of original sin; it leads to the transgression of boundaries, to polymorphous perversion and the pleasure principle. Given these parallels, obscenity indeed reveals itself as "heir to the religious tradition."

The spiritual awakening experienced by Charles Ryder at the end of Evelyn Waugh's *Brideshead Revisited: The Sacred and Profane Memoirs of Captain Charles Ryder* illustrates these ideas. Charles is a man who ultimately comes to reject the common sense of the reality principle, the realm he formerly termed "august" and "masculine." Now a captain in the British army, Charles previously told himself he would never return to the extensive country estate known as Brideshead, home of the Flyte family. He had visited Brideshead previously as a friend of the Flytes, an affluent, somewhat eccentric, but deeply religious family, their lives an admixture of opulence and Catholic devotion. To be sure, the Flytes adhered to the faith, yet were not without their share of alcoholics, adulterers, and other transgressors. At separate times in his life, Charles deeply loved two members of this family. In the company of the Flytes, he experienced great inspiration, a sense of the sub-

lime. A painter, he produced some of his best work while at Brideshead. Yet the family's emotional dramas and religious convictions
became too much for Charles; he felt overwhelmed by the driven
quality that expressed itself variously in different family members.
"I shall never go back," he told himself in an effort to be disabused
of the aesthetic, religious atmosphere of Brideshead—its "mumbo
jumbo," "witchcraft," and "tomfoolery"—which he would replace
with the common sense of the reality principle.

> I had left behind me—what? Youth? Adolescence? Romance? The
> conjuring stuff of these things, "the Young Magician's Compendi-
> um," that neat cabinet where the ebony wand had its place beside the
> billiard balls, the penny that folded double and the feather flowers
> that could be drawn into a hollow candle. "I have left behind illu-
> sion," I said to myself. "Henceforth I live in a world of three dimen-
> sions—with the aid of my five senses."[10]

However, *Brideshead Revisited* goes on to recount Charles's dis-
illusion with this belief in common sense, in three dimensions and
five senses. "I have since learned that there is no such world,"[11] he
states. Indeed he admits that, as a military man committed to law
and order, "at the age of thirty-nine I began to be old . . . something within me, long sickening, had quietly died."[12] But an unexpected visit to Brideshead with his military unit rekindles Charles's
dormant feelings. There, he recalls the passionate undercurrent that
had been present in all the Flytes, and in his relationships with them.
They themselves are not present in the house, but Charles revisits
those rooms in which he was a guest, and in which he painted. The
novel closes with his visit to the family chapel, where he is moved
by a red candle burning beside the tabernacle doors. He regains a
sense of the sublime:

> Something quite remote from anything the builders intended had come
> out of their work, and out of the fierce little human tragedy in which
> I had played; something none of us had thought about at the time: a
> small red flame—a beaten-copper lamp of deplorable design, relit
> before the beaten-copper doors of a tabernacle. . . . It could not have
> been lit but for the builders and the tragedians, and there I found it
> this morning, burning anew among the old stones. . . . I quickened
> my pace and reached the hut which served us for our ante-room. "You're
> looking unusually cheerful today," said the second-in-command.[13]

Hence Waugh's novel dramatizes one man's disaffection with

the reality principle and reawakening to the fact that it is negotiable, tentative, provisional. A more fluid realm lies beyond its reaches, a realm that can be experienced via spirituality, aesthetics, and of course the obscene. I believe that this desire for contrapuntal dedifferentiation resonates on an *instinctive* level (and is codified as "feminine" only within the confines of culture), and I wish to emphasize how it carries with it these powerful spiritual, aesthetic, and eschatological attributes. Obviously spirituality, death, rebirth, sexuality, and painting share some connection in Waugh's novel. All have feminine attributes, defy the reality principle, and release us from a worldly sense of time, for "eternity is the mode of unrepressed bodies."[14]

The Postmodern Feminine: The Untruth of Truth

In these pages, my primary task lies in highlighting the connection between the feminine and the obscene, and in demonstrating that the latter is integral to culture. Let me not fail to mention, however, that my analysis necessarily resonates with the metaphorical feminine's important intellectual standing within contemporary theoretical circles. It is well known that the feminine's resistance to *logos*, its defiance of common sense, and undermining of standardized systems of meaning renders it a celebrated metaphor for all that is negative, contrapuntal, and attuned to contemporary Continental philosophy. Indeed, I have already alluded to the fact that the feminine's defiance of organization and identity render it deconstructive. Hence what causes it to be obscene also explains its relation to Lacanian and Derridean epistemologies. The entire theoretical enterprise of positing human subjectivity in discursive rather than ontological terms, so integral to postmodernist and poststructuralist methods, dovetails with the maternal as a metaphor of opposition, subversion, and ideological counterpoint. In that it constantly resists the dictates of *logos* and forever announces the presence of the unconscious, the unknown, and the outside-of-meaning, the maternal metaphor resonates more with Nietzschean "wild wisdom" and dionysian creativity than with the systematic, appollonian realm of objective knowledge and the Cartesian *cogito*. Because the maternal defies deductive reasoning and hermeneutic closure, it bears resemblance to postmodernist and poststructuralist approaches to meaning. In Domna Stanton's words:

[T]he emphasis on female difference is part and parcel of the philosophy of difference that pervades contemporary thought.... [M]odernist
masters . . . have consistently coded as feminine that which exceeds
the grasp of the Cartesian subject—be it called nonknowledge or
nontruth, undecidability or supplementarity, even writing or the unconscious.[15]

In contemporary theoretical circles, the feminine becomes a
shorthand for all that is deconstructive, negative, and opposed to
phallogocentric logic. Jacques Derrida's criticism of the metaphysics of presence, for instance, leads him to wholeheartedly endorse
the metaphorical feminine, which defies *logos* and therefore cannot
posit a system of binary opposites. In its resistance to *logos*, the
feminine or maternal facilitates if not demands the deconstruction
of unified knowledge; meaning no longer remains fixed but is now
given play and made fluid, contextual, and contingent. Reading,
writing, interpreting, indeed the entire academic enterprise, now
assume a different agenda, at once more open-ended yet more urgently political. In the age of deconstruction, the professorial task
is not to convey the "central meaning" of revered texts from which
Western culture supposedly takes its bearings. Rather, its mission is
to shed light on the play and multiplicity of meanings contained in
such texts while highlighting the dangers of clinging to an established repertoire that, for all its value, necessarily excludes other
voices, positions, and meanings.

Derrida encapsulates the notion of the contrapuntal, multiplic-
itous, "feminine" nature of meaning in his term *différance*. Arguing
against the belief in an abiding, uniform system of truth present in
the spoken word rather than the written text, *différance* implies that
meaning remains forever "different" and "deferred." It is different
depending on who conveys it, to whom it is directed, how, and
when; it never remains fixed. It is "deferred" because there will
never be a totalized, all-inclusive interpretation of any communica-
tive act that precludes different readings. Texts make sense in relation to one another and in differing contexts. A single text, for instance, always produces various readings and has meaning only in
relation to other texts. Hence any interpretation thereof will always
comprise "different" and "deferred" interpretive moments. The concept of *différance* indeed exposes the danger of interpretive paradigms, paradigms that necessarily militate against the discursivity
and tenuousness of all meaning. Accordingly, it is only moments of

deconstructive analytic acumen, "feminine" moments standing out-side of and in opposition to the Western phallogocentric tradition, that Derrida celebrates for their philosophic integrity. He claims that such moments uphold intellectual rigor because they defy rigor, are more truthful because they defy truth.

Derrida's *Spurs: Nietzsche's Styles* aptly illuminates this reso-nance between feminism and deconstruction in its discussion of the feminine's contrapuntal, affirmative qualities. Such qualities are creative, joyful, and deeply insightful given that they take their bearings from outside the Western tradition's adherence to Carte-sian logic, interpretive closure, and the reality principle. Indeed, we could say that Freud's diminishing observations concerning wom-an's "retarding and restraining influence" upon civilization are em-phatically contradicted by Derrida. Unaligned with the reality prin-ciple, the feminine trope is life-affirming, at the center of every truly creative enterprise. It is precisely its status outside of meaning, in opposition to civilization, that renders the feminine powerful and desired. Derrida writes:

> There is no such thing as the essence of woman because woman averts, she is averted of herself. Out of the depths, endless and unfathom-able, she engulfs and distorts all vestige of essentiality, of identity, of property. And the philosophical discourse, blinded, founders on these shoals and is hurled down these depthless depths to its ruin. There is no such thing as the truth of woman, but it is because of that abyssal divergence of the truth, because that untruth is "truth." Woman is but one name for that untruth of truth. . . . That which will not be pinned down by truth is, in truth—*feminine*.[16]

Feminist scholars employing Derridean and Lacanian concepts, although numerous and variegated in their approaches, all adhere to a notion of the trope's positive qualities; all recognize the desir-ability of operating outside the system of binary opposition and fixed paradigms integral to phallogocentrism and prefer the feminine realm characterized by a multiplicity of meanings, dionysian irrationality, and a powerfully creative impulse. Such positive intellectual con-notations, which inform *l'écriture féminine*, thus dovetail with our discussion on obscenity, helping to further explain why reabsorp-tion into the maternal—into the dedifferentiated outside-of-mean-ing—constitutes a longed-for, meaningful experience in our culture, one that responds to instinct and is emotionally and intellectually charged.

Those authors particularly associated with *l'écriture féminine*
best illustrate the connection between the feminine, deconstruction,
and our understanding of the obscene. They are, among others, Julia
Kristeva, Hélène Cixous, Luce Irigaray, and Michèle Montrelay.
These authors' indebtedness to Lacan of course means that their
reading of repression and the unconscious remains alloyed to the
human acquisition of language. They argue that the inaugural loss
of the mother's body gives rise to the need for a signifying process
aimed at producing linguistic closure, at suturing the gap created
by this initial loss. Human speech therefore represents an effort to
dispel symbolic mediation, to find again that system of meaning
prior to language which knew no loss and was unscathed by the
reality principle.

We have seen already how Kristeva describes the sense of
power contained in the fluid, pre-oedipal imaginary devoid of lack.
For her, the maternal imaginary assumes primal, archaic connotations given its ability to countervail against identity's cohesion. It
is the space where human identity dissolves. Her term "abjection"
therefore refers to the strange and unsettling ambivalence which
characterizes all human identity. Abjection is ambivalent because it
acknowledges the diffused maternal underside of the socially constituted self, an underside which violently defies time and figura-
tion. Hence abjection resides not in a utopia but in an "atopia."

> The abject is the violence of mourning for an "object" that has always
> already been lost. The abject shatters the wall of repression and its
> judgments. It takes the ego back to its source on the abominable limits
> from which, in order to be, the ego has broken away—it assigns it a
> source in the non-ego, drive, and death. Abjection is a resurrection
> that has gone through death (of the ego). It is an alchemy that trans-
> forms death drive into a start of life, a new significance. . . . (Abjec-
> tion is) dazzling, unending, eternal . . . the absolute because primeval
> seat of the impossible—of the excluded, the outside-of-meaning, the
> abject. Atopia.[17]

Of course, the projects of Kristeva and other postmodernist
scholars committed to *l'écriture féminine* tend to differ from mine.
In general, they are more literary. Yet Kristeva illustrates our shared
theoretical framework by describing literature as an attempt to uncover the archaic maternal lost within us; as with all language, it is
"a race" toward the obscene feminine:

According to Borges the "object" of literature is . . . vertiginous and hallucinatory. . . . But what is it? Unless it be the untiring repetition of a drive, which, propelled by an initial loss, does not cease wandering, unsated, deceived, warped, until it finds its only stable object—death. . . . [T]he Borgesian race toward death . . . is contained in the chasm of the maternal cave.[18]

I thus see strong parallels between Kristeva's notion of an abject atopia and my understanding of obscenity, especially in light of her insistence that we desire a maternal matrix like that contained in the imaginary even as we recognize its abjection. She too understands the feminine as countervailing, contrapuntal, unaligned with culture's dictates but responding to the death drive, resisting the claims of *logos*. In Elizabeth Grosz's words: "(Kristeva's) [a]bjection is one of the few avowals of the death drive, an undoing of the processes constituting the subject."[19] Kristeva thus upholds an intellectual reabsorption back into the maternal, a flight from the authoritative pretenses of phallogocentrism. She applauds the efforts of literary and artistic expression to apprehend abjection, to uncover the feminine outside-of-meaning commensurate with Lacan's Imaginary. While this enterprise remains grounded in impulses and drives—"propelled by an initial loss," the loss that inspires Lacanian desire—it nevertheless becomes an intellectual activity. She celebrates writing, painting, music, and literary and cultural criticism. Kristeva's work therefore clarifies how postmodernist scholars understand the feminine in ways similar to our own. She seeks to uncover the abject maternal so obfuscated by patriarchal culture and to make plain its unsettling powers.

Having thus examined the feminine's prominence in postmodernist circles, we have further clarified the intellectual weight that it carries. I now wish to return to its relationship to obscenity, situating my analysis in a clearly defined political, sociohistoric context. Specifically, I wish to move from a theoretical investigation into why the obscene is feminine or maternal, to an elucidation of this claim in the context of the contemporary West, especially the United States. Indeed, our investigation into the cultural archetype of the feminine is greatly enhanced when situated within a specific cultural context. This is because I believe there are certain characteristics of the Western cultural and political scene that render obscenity a particularly charged issue, characteristics that are perhaps most pronounced in the United States, given our tremendous emphasis on individualism, the uniqueness of American pluralism, and our changing status as a world power. Specifically, these characteristics include the intense privatization of meaning, the resultant expectations we hold vis-à-vis our discrete identities with their privately forged meanings, and the fact that, at least since the 1960s, some of our most powerful cultural archetypes have undergone renegotiation. Let me examine these statements concerning our cultural specificity more closely.

CHAPTER FOUR

The Contribution
of Critical Theory

We have seen that certain schools of psychoanalytic thought buttress the assertion that our discontinuous, individuated identities play
themselves out against the backdrop of an abiding desire to experience continuity, to enter a realm wherein our discrete existences have
no status and the boundaries of self are suspended. This desire is
explained in terms of a basic human drive, thanatos. An innate
impulse toward homeostasis, thanatos assures our longing for an
unmediated relationship to the world and to meaning, a relationship
that is feminine or maternal.

Obscenity responds to this longing, and so performs a crucial
social function. It recalls the distinction between the primal, maternal realm of psychic death and continuity and the orderly, phallic,
taboo-ridden sphere of discontinuity; hence it remains alloyed to the
life and death impulses. If one accepts drive theory, one accepts
that the obscene finds itself enmeshed in the union of these drives.
Obscenity announces the longing for a Nirvana-like homeostasis
even as it satisfies the erotic urge. Evoking the dialectic between
the pleasure and reality principles, obscenity highlights the socially
sanctioned yet tenuous hold of the latter over the former. Indeed,
by its very nature, the illicit feminine calls into question the reality
principle, drawing attention to the variability of its cultural and historical manifestations. I acknowledge the reality principle's role in
advancing human civilization yet insist on its provisional, negotiable nature.

If the reality principle is indeed provisional, do human drives
and impulses concatenate themselves variously within different so-

ciohistorical settings? If the reality principle remains pliable, is repression itself mutable? These questions are of special interest to me given my claim that the provisional, negotiable nature of the reality principle directly influences how persons experience the basic drives, and therefore repression, within given sociohistoric contexts. Such questions therefore have bearing on our investigation into why obscenity is currently such a charged issue in American culture.

Authors such as Herbert Marcuse, Norman O. Brown, and Jessica Benjamin have argued that cultural, economic, and political specificities greatly influence how human beings respond to basic drives and impulses; empirical factors, they insist, determine human repression. Although only Marcuse is formally associated with critical theory, all three attempt to situate psychoanalytic premises within historical and cultural confines, thereby forcing investigations into the human psyche to be empirically grounded. Simply put, these authors attempt a synthesis of psychoanalytic and socioeconomic spheres, arguing that human drives concatenate themselves in relation to the material givens of a culture. Hence their writings analyze human sexual impulses—their expression, sublimation, and repression—in relation to those empirical factors contributing to the actual fabric of society. Included among these are a society's degree of industrialization, level of production, economic scarcity or opulence, and distribution of wealth, as well as the class relations that this distribution generates. Twentieth-century Americans, these authors would argue, do not experience repression in the same way as did Americans living a century ago. The enormous industrial, technological, and economic advances this country has made, together with the relative affluence these have produced, generate a repression different from that in the nineteenth century. As in other industrialized Western nations, the material base of American culture dictates a repression specific to capitalism, one that, we shall see, frequently remains hidden by our putative commitment to sexual freedom and movements of liberation.

Because we cannot discuss the obscene in ways divorced from the larger cultural arena in which it articulates itself, I wish to reopen this discussion on the mutability of drives. I undertake this project—one already pursued by the above-mentioned authors—with a view toward understanding why, at this moment in history, obscenity constitutes such a highly charged and avidly debated topic in American culture. Why this intense discussion of who controls the reality principle, who can proclaim from the beyond? Why this highly politicized debate over the obscene, which is so primal, so opposed to civilization, so seemingly removed from the arena in which politics plays itself out?

I believe that obscenity reveals two things about American culture. First and most generally, it reveals a conflict between the innate human desire for continuity and our ideological commitment to individualism, progress, technology, and science. Second and more specifically, the topic unveils an immediate need in American culture to reassert control over the reality principle, which—now in a state of flux for a variety of reason—must be harnessed and controlled with redoubled effort.

In this chapter, I will discuss the conflict between innate human drives and Western culture's ideological commitments. Specifically, I will highlight how the search for continuity is displaced onto the discontinuous realm, causing us to expect too much from our individual identities. The following chapter will illustrate this second point more fully and discuss it in terms of a threatened, fluxuating American hegemony.

Eros and Civilization: Mutable and Immutable Human Instincts

I accept the psychoanalytic premise that civilization is predicated on repression, that taboo constitutes the sine qua non of human culture. Moreover, along with the above-mentioned authors, I insist that this repression be analyzed within the context of historical specificities—social, cultural, political, economic. Eros and thanatos must be apprehended in keeping with the material givens of a culture, for such empirical factors greatly influence how we experience internal drives. For our purposes, this means that psychoanalytic precepts must be considered within the context of advanced capitalism, a social state of advanced industrial and technological development wherein monopoly capital prevails. Fusing these analytic approaches allows us to consider the drives specifically under capitalism and to then apply this consideration to our discussion of obscenity. I believe that a theoretical exploration of the drives under capitalism has been carefully undertaken in Marcuse's influential *Eros and Civilization: A Philosophical Inquiry into Freud*, a text that also links the drives' mutability to our conflicted feelings toward "the feminine."

The power behind Marcuse's argument lies in his ability to conceptualize broadly the human experience of toil and suffering in ways specific to advanced capitalism. Although this suffering is temporarily relieved by pleasure and gratification, Marcuse argues that only a rearranged economic base can meaningfully alleviate what is a necessary by-product of most capitalist systems: namely, our thwarted human instincts, our impoverished humanity, and the distorted manner in which we experience eros and thanatos. Marcuse begins by distinguishing "basic" from "surplus" repression. The former coincides with Freud's now familiar notion of repression as integral to civilization. Civilization's need to identify taboo generates prohibitions, granting the reality principle license to harness and control basic human impulses. In this way, basic repression gives rise to *ananke*, the economy of scarcity that accompanies repression and dictates that human beings cannot live according to the pleasure principle, but must internalize a self-policing tendency that acclimates them to culture. Basic repression mandates that the "maternal" feminine realm of pleasure, plenitude, and dedifferentiation must yield to the organized, phallogocentric, "paternal" realm that imposes law and order; this allows civilization to flourish. In adopting this Freudian precept, Marcuse concedes that basic repression is essential to human culture. He thus imbues it with transhistorical connotations.

"Surplus repression," on the other hand, refers to a category of human repression that is not transhistorical. Rather, it emanates from the specificities of capitalist society, from the particular mode of production that prevails in advanced industrialized cultures. Hence surplus repression is commensurate with a society's level of industrialization, the prevalence of private ownership, its distribution of wealth, quality of life, relationship between government, business, and labor, and so on. Marcuse stresses that surplus repression exists as the offspring of late capitalism; were the material givens of a capitalist culture altered, surplus repression would change or be eliminated along with them.

What characterizes this form of repression, internalized by persons living in advanced capitalist cultures? It is the conceptualization and treatment of the human body as essentially an instrument of labor, something made to produce, perform, toil, and be remunerated. It is an organizing of the body that distrusts and fears the feminine, and consequently submits to *logos*. Under capitalism, the body is an agent of production; hence the human person is primarily conceived of as a worker, a money-earner, a career-seeker answering to the demands and dictates of capitalism. Indeed, according to Marcuse, this form of production conflates human existence with human toil, and the means to life too frequently become confused with life itself. Here we clearly witness the impact of Marxian precepts on Marcuse's thought, for it was Marx who originally observed that, under capitalism, the means to life frequently become conflated with life itself. This conflation—which casts the human body as an instrument of labor, holding pleasure, dedifferentiation, and the feminine at bay—contributes to that labor's being "alienated": excessively exigent, physically exhausting, too frequently unsatisfying, demoralizing, and undignified. In addition to confusing money with life, then, alienated labor estranges human beings from the commodities they produce, estranges them from one another, and indeed from themselves—from their own human, creative potential. In Marx's words, this form of human toil

> is the relation of the worker to his own activity as an alien activity not belonging to him; it is activity as suffering, strength as weakness, begetting as emasculating, the worker's *own* physical and mental energy, his personal life . . . as an activity which is turned against him, neither depends on nor belongs to him. Here we have *self-estrangement. . . .*[1]

Marcuse targets these dehumanizing aspects of capitalist production in his analysis of surplus repression. Consequently, he observes that less-developed, largely agricultural societies generally impose an attenuated form of this repression on their inhabitants as compared to Western industrialized countries. Although he does not argue for the simple elimination of capitalist production (which he recognizes as having numerous and diverse incarnations), Marcuse does maintain that restructuring production according to more collectivist principles—principles focused as much on the quality of life as on the economy's competitive edge—will vitiate if not eliminate surplus repression, thereby redirecting the very manner in which human beings internalize prohibition and experience basic drives. Within a more collectivist system, human beings will feel part of what Marx terms the "species being." We recall that his vision of a humane society was one in which a person could "hunt in the morning, fish in the afternoon, rear cattle in the evening, criticize after dinner . . . without ever becoming hunter, fisherman, shepherd or critic."[2] In such a society, people will thus no longer be alienated from one another and from themselves, but will discover a less repressed, more "erotic" sense of reality; they will not be victimized by the emotional and spiritual exhaustion that accompanies long working hours that garner them mere subsistence. In its lessened repression, the resultant erotic sense of reality will admit not a duality but a dialectic between being and nonbeing, that same dialectic to which the obscene now gives expression. Lessened repression will dispel the current ambivalence that inheres between the drives in favor of their fusion, what Brown calls humanity's "immortal project of recovering its own childhood."[3] This will allow the obscene maternal to infiltrate culture's adherence to "august" "masculine" tenets, giving voice to the dionysian pleasure principle now held in check by the apollonian realm.

Proposing that we abolish "not labor, but the organization of . . . human existence into an instrument of labor,"[4] Marcuse thus argues for the feasibility of a nonrepressive reality principle. Indeed throughout *Eros and Civilization*, he insists that the basic human instincts can prevail in a manner less antagonistic to the interests of civilization than suggested by Freud. Consequently, where there is less repression, there is more continuity. Human experience is less self-contained, less self-referential within the confines of our private "identities." Hence thanatos—the retrograde, conservative, life-preserving impulse characterized by repetition-compulsion—could yield more easily to the life-affirming, creative instincts of eros were our culture less repressed. The ambivalent dualism of the drives would be resolved in favor of a more dialectical relationship, one recognizing that being and nonbeing are in fact part of each other. Brown writes:

Freud's ontological postulate of the innate ambivalence of instincts . . . is contradicted by the empirical theorem of a first, pre-ambivalent stage in infancy. And the fixation of that first pre-ambivalent experience commits mankind to the unconscious project of overcoming the instinctual ambivalence which is his actual condition and of restoring the unity of opposites that existed in childhood. . . .[5]

The newly sexualized body would internalize less of a conflict between id, ego, and superego; consequently, it would be less genitally organized. No longer conceived as an instrument of labor, the newly eroticized body would more closely approximate polymorphous perversion. It would be freed from the tyranny of the genitals, so to speak, and enjoy a more diffused sensuousness. Indeed, the reorganization of the human body away from repressive mandates—a reorganization breeding a new type of eroticism under the sway of the female pleasure principle—is perhaps the most significant consequence of the advocated social rearrangement.

Were the distinction between pleasure and toil attenuated and diffused, Marcuse argues, gratification would no longer be so delayed and rationed an experience; the reorganized human body would find parallels between "work pleasure" and libidinal pleasure. Importantly, Marcuse does not advocate promiscuity but a redirecting of the basic drives in ways attuned to human need. He terms the mature, resexualized body "genitofugal":

> Non-repressive order is possible only if the sex instincts can, by virtue of their own dynamic and under changed existential and societal conditions, generate lasting erotic relations among mature individuals. We have to ask whether the sex instincts, after the elimination of all surplus-repression, can develop a "libidinal rationality" which is not only compatible with but even promotes progress toward higher forms of civilized freedom. . . . And this "cultural" trend in the libido seems to be *genitofugal*, that is to say, *away* from genital supremacy toward the erotization of the entire organism.[6]

A culture lacking in surplus repression is thus deemed "mature." It is one that reaps the benefits of capitalist development while stemming the latter's tendency to thwart the human subject.

In disagreeing with Freud's premise that human sensuality and pleasure militate against the interests of civilization, Marcuse's analysis dovetails with my inquiry into the obscene in many ways. For instance, in distinguishing the pleasure and reality principles, whose relationship he seeks to renegotiate, he explicitly uses the terms "feminine" and "masculine." The former, of course, denotes all that threatens to undermine the progress and authority of civilization. The "female principle," as he calls it, evokes pleasure, satiation, and sensuality. This principle is anthropomorphized in the mythical figures of Pandora, Orpheus, and Narcissus. In Greek myth, these persons are troublemaking, self-indulgent, and pleasure-seeking; like the maternal metaphor, they are envoys of otherness, representatives of the contrapuntal. This resonates with Marcuse's statement, quoted earlier, that fear of a castrating, punishing father is actually preceded by fear of an engulfing pre-oedipal mother, symbol of the fact that the pleasure principle can swallow us up by annihilating our discrete identities. "[I]n the world of the reality principle," Marcuse writes, "Pandora, the female principle, sexuality and pleasure, appear as a curse—disruptive, destructive. . . . The beauty of the woman, and the happiness she promises are fatal in the work-world of civilization."[7] Hence the feminine is enemy to civilization also in myth. This is how Orpheus and Narcissus, although male, can join in the feminine enterprise of undermining the reality principle:

> Orpheus and Narcissus (like Dionysus to whom they are akin . . .) stand for a very different reality. They have not become the culture-heroes of the Western world: theirs is the image of joy and fulfillment, the voice which does not command but sings; the gesture which offers and receives; the deed which is peace and ends the labor of conquest; the liberation from time which unites man with god, man with nature.[8]

If these figures are envoys of feminine otherness, uncommitted to suffering and toil, then who are the culture-heroes of the Western world? According to Marcuse, Prometheus stands prominently among them. As one who submits to a more masculine ethos, he symbolizes progress and productivity, "the unceasing effort to master life,"[9] to advance human civilization at all costs. In that he disobeys the gods in order to champion human progress, the figure of Prometheus fuses the categories of culture and toil, achievement and pain, suggesting that one may not be obtained without the other. In a world where Prometheus is hero, progress remains inextricably linked to repression. "He symbolizes productiveness, the unceasing effort to master life," writes Marcuse of Prometheus, "but, in his productivity, blessing and curse, progress and toil are inextricably intertwined. Prometheus is the archetype-hero of the performance principle."[10]

In Western culture, work is frequently arduous and alienated, so rarely pleasurable; it is a culture that construes the feminine realm as dangerous and contrapuntal, something to be held in check. Marcuse's own opposition to this conceptual fusion and subsequent insistence that eros and civilization need not be antagonistic lead him to quote Baudelaire: "True civilization does not lie in gas, nor in steam, nor in turntables. It lies in the reduction of the traces of original sin."[11] Hence the hallmark of a humane, mature culture is lessened repression, not advanced technology. It is a changed disposition toward the human body, not increased mastery over culture. Reducing these traces means giving play to the primal, archaic maternal. It means articulating the obscene feminine as something necessary to culture. In this way, Marcuse's "mature" culture is mature precisely because it admits the feminine; its commitment to dialectics precludes its submission to *logos*, to rationalism, and to binary opposition.

Mature Civilization and the Regenerated Flesh

Lifting the veil of repression thus makes contact with the continuous, dedifferentiated realm prevailing prior to the reality principle. It hastens our return to "an old state of things," a state devoid of the distinction between work and play, one in which the reality principle has been unmasked as an ideological tool serving the purposes of a repressive social order. It produces not a childish regression but our advancement toward a mature state wherein labor is never alienated, and the basic drives are not pitted against civilization. With human instinct and human culture no longer at odds, repression will be lessened and the unconscious made conscious. "The axis of world history is to make conscious the unconscious," Brown writes.[12] Importantly, this would allow our recognition of the tenuousness of the reality principle, a recognition that breeds a poetic, metaphorical, "erotic" sense of reality. For if the reality principle itself is tenuous, so are our socially conditioned, culturally acclimated selves. With our identities exposed as discursive creations, our entire perception of the world becomes more fluid and equivocal. The boundaries between subject and object break down as the distinction between psychic reality and empirical truth reorients itself. Arguing that our "identities" merely seek to recreate the lost mother—that initial "object" whose loss inaugurated the reality principle—Brown insists that "[s]chizophrenics are suffering from the truth."[13] Such an awareness ushers in the liberating recognition that our differentiated, repressed, genitally organized selves are merely provisional.

[P]ersonality is a social fiction . . . internal reality is truth. . . . The antinomy between mind and body, word and deed, speech and silence, [must be] overcome. Everything is only a metaphor; there is only poetry.[14]

Assuming a disposition vis-à-vis reality that is maternal rather than phallogocentric, metaphorical, and poetic, rather than repressive and instrumentally rational, would thus reconnect human civilization to the human body. Only by pursuing a dedifferentiated relationship to reality can we reduce repression and fulfill our desire "for a recovery of the body from which culture alienates us."[15] For if civilization's dependence on taboo has traditionally bred a genitally organized body, letting go of that organization can only reunite us with our polymorphous perverse pasts. Letting go can help us rediscover an unmediated relationship to the world and help return us to "an old state of things," a state less invested in the self, which consequently admits a sense of timelessness. Yet Western culture's commitment to secular humanism—to individualism, the reality principle, the protection of private property—buttresses the "fiction" of the possessive, assertive individual, and thus goes against this dictum. Once again we recall Marcuse's statement that a culture's reality principle stands commensurate with its fear of the feminine, which must be held at bay. However, even under present circumstances and despite our fear of the feminine, we do try to renegotiate this reconnection to the body. One way is via the obscene, which allows us to retreat from boundaries and defy the reality principle, hence its integral status to culture.

Wim Wenders's *Wings of Desire* dramatizes such an effort to reconnect human civilization to the body, to give expression to the feminine pleasure principle, which recognizes the dialectic between being and nonbeing. The film tells the tale of an angel, Damiel, who wishes to become human. Damiel frequents the city of Berlin with his fellow angel, Cassiel. Together, they bear witness to the intense spiritual longings of Berliners. The angels arrive at an automobile accident and hear the victim's dying thoughts; they listen to the grieving self-reproach of a man about to throw himself from a building; they follow an elderly man nostalgic for times gone by. The affinities between Wenders's project and my theoretical precepts are established early in the film. This happens when the angels listen to the internal monologue of a woman riding a bicycle who has recognized the fictitious nature of reality: "At last mad. At last no longer alone. At last mad. At last redeemed. At last insane. At last at peace."

Although very few people can see the angels—sometimes children can, and other angels—Damiel and Cassiel try to assuage human suffering and offer solace to the despairing. Deeply compassionate, the angels' existence is entirely spiritual; hence they are timeless creatures whose corporal appearance is not really material. They must "remain spirit"; their duty is to "observe, collect, testify, preserve." Damiel's deepest desire, however, is to depart this spiritual existence and become human. He wants to possess a human body, to live in it and know the world through it. He wants to be excited not only by ideas but by "the curve of a neck," or "by a meal." Most important for our purposes is the fact that Damiel does not perceive physical sensation as antithetical to his own spiritual existence; as one who already proclaims from the beyond, who knows dedifferentiation, the angel does not view continuity and discontinuity as antagonistic categories. To him, physical sensation and sexual desire appear to provide human beings with a form of knowledge that purely spiritual beings cannot grasp. He complains to Cassiel:

It's great to live only by the spirit. To testify day by day for eternity only to the spiritual side of people. But sometimes I get fed up with my spiritual existence. Instead of forever hovering above, I'd like to feel that there's some weight to my existence, to end my eternity and bind me to earth.

The angel thus seeks to uncover a lost unity between body and spirit. What he wants is to be able to "take (his) shoes off under the table," "to come home after a long day, like Philip Marlowe, and feed the cat." This illustrates a longing to dispel the antinomy between body and mind supported by the reality principle; it explains why a "yearning for death itself" might well be "voluptuous."

Damiel indeed acquires a body; Cassiel witnesses his passage from spirit into matter and interprets it largely as an act of courage. With this development in its storyline, Wenders's film dramatizes Brown's assertion concerning the bodily meaning of history, his assertion that redemption is corporeal. Brown writes:

[C]onsciousness—Christian or psychoanalytical, or Dionysian—terminates in the body, remains faithful to the earth. The dreamer awakes not from a body but to a body. Not an ascent from body to spirit, but the descent of spirit into body: incarnation not sublimation. Hence to find the true meaning of history is to find the bodily meaning. Christ, the fulfillment, is not an abstract idea but a human body. All fulfillment is carnal, *carnaliter adimpleri*.[16]

After his first night of love, Damiel affirms "Only the amaze-
ment about the two of us . . . made a human being of me. I know
now what no angel knows."

With this, I do not mean to imply that sexual experience is the
only experience that challenges the reality principle. All of the dimensions of what I have termed the maternal—currently harnessed
and controlled by the paternal, phallogocentric realm of culture—
performs this function. And were our culture to apprehend the feminine realm more fully, I believe we would experience a newly eroticized existence, one less constrained by a reality principle that is
fearful of the maternal. We would understand our deep need for
obscenity, so necessary in that it challenges our internalized repression and calls into question the limits of culture.

Yet Western culture thwarts an apprehension of the feminine,
and instead fosters high levels of repression. Especially in the twen-
tieth century, our society fails to buttress the notions of continuity
and dedifferentiation; steeped in the legacy of the humanist tradition, committed to individualism, progress, and technology, it fa-
vors the work-oriented ethos of the reality principle. For instance,
in *The Overworked American: The Unexpected Decline of Leisure*,[17]
Juliet Schor has recently argued that Americans now spend consid-
erably more time at work than they did previously. In order to earn
a living, they work harder to maintain households in which they
spend less time. They put in longer hours at the office and take
shorter holidays and fewer personal days. Hence Prometheus is increasingly our cultural hero as our bodies are more fully codified
as instruments of labor. This work-oriented individualism has been
described as contributing to our sense of deadness, isolation, and
unreality. In Jessica Benjamin's words,

> [T]he individualistic emphasis on strict boundaries between self and
> others promotes a sense of isolation and unreality. Paradoxically, the
> individualism of our culture seems to make it more difficult to accept
> an other's independence and to experience the other person as real.
> In turn, it is difficult to connect with others as living erotic beings,
> to feel erotically alive oneself. Violence acquires its importance in
> erotic fantasy as an expression of the desire to break out of this numbing
> encasement. . . . I believe that we are facing unbearably intensified
> privatization and discontinuity, unrelieved by expressions of continu-
> ity . . . we are facing a crisis of male rationality. . . .[18]

Our numbing encasement illustrates the manner in which our
culture supports a high level of repression, keeping the erotic drive

pitted against the interests of civilization. Our focus on discontinuity remains too great. We champion individual endeavor, the advancement of civilization, and culture's control over nature; we repudiate the maternal, which appears as an archaic category capable of arresting civilization's forward motion. As a whole, then, our culture concurs with the larger implications of Freud's statement concerning woman's enemy status. In that we deny our impulse toward dedifferentiation, differentiation is overvalued. Our culture does not support the tension that must inhere between our individuated, acclimated selves and our continuous, unindividuated existences. There is too little continuity for human beings to support the paradox between the life and death instincts: Instead of being brought to life by a sense of dedifferentiation, we are deadened by the increased pressure experienced in the differentiated realm. We expect too much from our privately forged selves, wrongly convinced that the feminine is a dangerous enemy rather than a necessary envoy of otherness.

Hence the distinction between self and other, mediated and unmediated, and psychic and empirical realms remains insufficiently attenuated. There is no dialectical relationship, rather binary opposition. Failing to support the paradox between the life and death instincts causes us to cast them as starkly antagonistic. In our repudiation of the maternal, we are unable to sustain the necessary tension between eros and thanatos.

How exactly does binary opposition, this exaltation of *logos*, play itself out? I believe that the absence of continuity—of the Nirvana principle, of the self joined to a larger whole in defiance of everyday boundaries—breeds a conflict that *seeks resolution in the realm of discontinuity.* Our inability to diffuse the boundaries of self leads to nothing other than an exalted belief in the self: its cause, its meaning, the importance of its specificities. We champion the individual, yet this enterprise merely seeks to make up for a lack of continuity. A yearning for the continuous realm thus brings heightened expectation to the discontinuous one.

What forms do these expectations take? We expect feelings of plenitude, closure, and resolution from the discontinuous realm, feelings that the continuous realm alone can supply. Personality, identity, a raised consciousness, the longing for personal and sexual liberation are examples of how, in our culture, discontinuity strives to make up for the absence of continuity, to perform its role for it. Indeed, since the sixties, the emphasis on liberation, self-awareness, and self-expression—buttressed by the popularity of various schools of psychology, movements of liberation, and attention to the many forms of difference—has promised to deliver a sense of fulfillment and self-completion to those who take seriously our attention to the self. For instance, it has frequently been said that in the sixties, Americans read magazines entitled *Life* and *Look*; in the seventies we read *Psychology Today*; and in the eighties and nineties we read *Self*. We used to go to concerts and films; now, thanks to the VCR, we have the choice of attending these publically or watching them on video in the privacy of our living rooms. Understanding the self, expressing the self, believing it to be its own raison d'être, deploring the extent to which it is thwarted by society: These mandates so characteristic of our epoch exemplify the high expectations we place on the differentiated realm—the realm of "personality." To me, this aspect of our culture evokes pathos, for it never achieves what it searches for. We want the self to deliver things that can only be attained by transgressing the boundaries of self, be it through obscene expression, art, music, sexuality, or spirituality, etc.

Let me restate my earlier claim, however, that not all such attempts at transgressing boundaries succeed. As mentioned earlier, for instance, pornography frequently fails to affirm the power of the obscene; instead, it simply appropriates sexual representation in ways too aligned with *logos* to be truly contrapuntal. In the language of critical theory, then, we can say that pornography's manipulation by the culture industry frequently destroys its negative dimension, rendering it insufficiently "obscene."[19] Yet our consumption of pornography bespeaks our continuing hope that the realm of *logos* might deliver, that it might fulfill our deep-seated needs. We are wrongly looking for continuity in the discontinuous realm.

My argument in no way seeks to undermine those political causes organized around issues of human identity. Race, class, gender, sexual identity, and sexual orientation remain topics urgently in need of attention within the context of Western societies, societies that are traditionally Eurocentric, male supremacist, homophobic, anti-Semitic, and so forth. I wholeheartedly support feminism, racial equality, gay and lesbian liberation, and the struggle against all forms of bigotry and discrimination. It is not the attention to difference found in these causes that I caution against. Nor do I deny the value in movements of liberation that can indeed loosen the grip of an antiquated ethos. Rather, it is the far-reaching, august quality of the rewards promised by these causes that I question. I disagree that the differentiated realm can ever provide the sense of plenitude and closure that belongs uniquely to dedifferentiation. Hence I concur with Shane Phelan's argument, pursued in her *Identity Politics: Lesbian Feminism and the Limits of Community*. Phelan insists that, by promising "truth," "freedom," and other metaphysical rewards, identity politics produce their own particular breed of danger. Specifically, such politics posit essentializing claims that, I would argue, run counter to the dialectical tension of drive theory. Well-meaning in their fight against oppression, they hope that individual identity will produce a sense of closure. Phelan recommends that we not take this search for closure too seriously: "The opposite of oppression in this sense is, not truth or respect, but humor or lightheartedness—the humor that comes from seeing all categories, all explanations, all identities as provisional."[20]

Identities can never truly satiate the intense longing they seek to appease, for they are temporary, mutable, too ensconced within the differentiated realm to resonate with the abject maternal, the death drive. Identity is a discursive creation, a fiction; because the social self necessarily answers to the dictates of the reality principle, it can never delve deeply enough to experience the Nirvana principle. This is why Brown characterizes the politics of the existing social realm as "juvenile delinquency."[21] Only when the self is bypassed, transcended, denied can this sense of closure be achieved; only when we acknowledge the abject maternal, the outside-of-meaning, can we proclaim from the beyond. Hence obscenity, forever recalling taboo and our ability to transgress its boundaries, remains a necessary category within culture, reaching deeply to our core.

This inability of discontinuity to perform the function of continuity causes the quest for sexual liberation to appear somewhat farcical. This is not to imply that current levels of repression should be sustained; rather, it states that our efforts to lower them have been misguided. It is now some twenty-five years since we began to speak of sexual liberation in the West, of overturning the vestiges of the Victorian era, thus disburdening ourselves of our repressive pasts and finally allowing our sexual "identities" to breathe freely. The promise of this liberation—which organizes itself variously around such topics as sexual orientation, sexual identity, women's liberation, gay and lesbian liberation, the state and sexuality, reproductive rights, and of course obscenity—argues that once lib-

eration is achieved, an important facet of our identities will experience a long-awaited closure, a sense of completion that a puritani-
cal strain has disallowed. Again, I support the visibility and continued success of each of these causes; it is the promise of fulfillment
and closure that I question. It suggests that a feeling of wholeness
will be restored to the individual once sexuality is finally liberated.
Our "sexual identities" will supposedly deliver a sense of satiation
paralleling orgasm, something Kuhn aptly terms "the big O." The
champions of sexual liberation thus promise that a fully articulated
sexual identity will deliver a complete individual, just as capitalism, in its promotion of commodities that aim to satisfy deeply,
promises to do the same. Yet I contend that this completion is not
feasible via the discontinuous realm, but only via the experience of
continuity.

Given that sexual identity and liberation belong in the differentiated realm, moreover, the effort to comprehend and achieve these
states appeals to the individual's instrumental reason and fact-find-
ing skills. Ours is indeed an age of information: having it, understanding it, transmitting it. If knowledge is power, information constitutes a most valued form of that knowledge. Thus it is believed
that what is needed to achieve the stated liberation is information
regarding human sexuality, information produced by what Foucault
terms *scientia sexualis*. This is factual information that, it is argued,
should be freely exchanged, openly discussed, professionally sound,
approved by experts. The highly equivocal realm of human sexuality now submits to diagnostics. When asked what constitutes the
most overrated sex advice, Dr. Ruth Westheimer responds: "There's
no such thing. You can never get enough advice."[22] Of course, the
commitment to discussing such topics as rape, sexual abuse, preg-
nancy, and AIDS—especially among teenagers and others likely to
be uninformed—needs no defending. But I am speaking about a
different kind of information exchange, one with a very different
purpose and ideological ramifications.

Since the sixties, it has been believed that the ability to speak
about sexuality will reveal some hidden truth, some important but
undisclosed reality about our sexual existences that has bearing on
our "true" identities. Speaking openly about sex, it is felt, can thus
aid in producing the sense of closure that sexuality is reputed to
bestow. Thus the proliferation of discourse surrounding sexuality
putatively hastens its liberating potential. Inasmuch as this proliferation operates in the discontinuous realm, however, it can never fully

succeed. The quest is misguided. Woody Allen recogniz
thos that our incessant chatter invokes. Many of his film
this sad undercurrent in contemporary life, which, if viewed in a
certain light, can appear humorous. In *Manhattan*, for instance, Mary
is an erudite woman convinced that her ability to speak analytical-
ly about sexual experience, and indeed about everything, will contribute to her happiness among New York artists and intellectuals.
She maintains that her pet dachshund, Waffles, functions as a penis
substitute. Yet despite her garrulous analysis, she wonders at times
about all this detailed scrutiny of her sexual "identity"; in despairing moments, she admits to being "all fucked up."

Why hasn't our effusive, free-flowing discussion about sexuality proved useful? Why haven't our sexual identities delivered? In
sum, why are we still *talking* about repression?

Our sexual identities haven't delivered because we expect the
discontinuous realm to produce a sense of closure and plenitude that,
by definition, it cannot yield. The bodily experience of orgasm, the
feeling of freedom and agency that come with sexual exploration,
the ability to talk openly about sex: Pleasurable and important as
these are, they can only approximate the sense of release that accompanies an undermining of the reality principle and a realization
of its provisional, tenuous hold over human life. The ability to transgress discrete, everyday boundaries, to experience the outside-of-
meaning, to "go right up into the ass of death" and "find the womb
of fear" in fact constitutes the deliverance needed. The dialectical
union between the life and death drives dictates our need for reabsorption back into dedifferentiation, back into the maternal, feminine realm, forever an enemy of civilization. Only there do we return to the body, as it were, and discover a more poetic reality. How
effectively we maneuver this reabsorption remains enmeshed within the material givens of the present culture, not in our ability to
throw off the putative vestiges of a distant forerunner.

With Foucault, then, I believe that our incessant discussion of
sexual liberation unwittingly sustains a high level of repression inasmuch as it keeps us preoccupied with our private identities. Foucault insists that our obsession with sexual liberation casts us as
"other Victorians." Instead of never discussing sex, we discuss it
all the time, we exchange information. All our talk simply unveils
a similar, perhaps greater unease with sexuality than supposedly
prevailed in Victorian times: "A suspicious mind might wonder if
taking so many precautions in order to give the history of sex such

an impressive filiation does not bear traces of the same old prud-
ishness."[23] We are perhaps more obsessed with our putative repression than we are truly repressed. Foucault comments:

> The question I would like to pose is not, Why are we repressed? but
> rather, Why do we say, with so much passion and so much resentment
> against our most recent past, against our present, and against our-
> selves, that we are repressed. . . . It is certainly legitimate to ask why
> sex was associated with sin for such a long time . . . but we must also
> ask why we burden ourselves today with so much guilt for having
> once made sex a sin.[24]

Foucault's critique, of course, emanates from his disbelief in
psychoanalysis and other scientifically oriented disciplines supposedly concerned with human health, justice, and freedom. Given his
critique of these premises, the theoretical disjunctures that separate
his writings from my own cannot be reconciled; I remain too
grounded in drive theory to truly parallel Foucault's analysis. However, there exists an obvious consensus in our undertakings concerning the great investment in sexual liberation that so characterizes
Western culture.

Western culture remains committed to an individualistic, competitive, profit-oriented ethos characteristic of monopoly capitalism;
it remains organized by a bourgeois state that jealously guards its
corridors of power. Although this ethos has not eradicated all cor-
porate structures and collectivist organizations, such units operate
against the backdrop of political, economic, and industrial machin-
eries essentially mired in the fundamentals of classical liberalism
and the humanist tradition, on whose theoretical base most Western
nations stand. Certainly these statements accurately describe American culture. The American heritage borrows directly from the English and French enlightenments and openly professes its long-standing defence of human rights, individualism, a free-market economy,
and the importance of instrumental reason. Indeed, the United States
remains committed to the humanist tradition. Individualism, progress,
advanced technology, competition, free enterprise, and free speech
all weigh heavily on the American political and cultural scene. Seeking to uphold the Enlightenment tradition, we thus strive to protect
the individual's right to life, liberty, and the pursuit of happiness,
with "happiness" generally interpreted as the acquisition of money,
property, or social status.

American culture thus joins the material mandates of laissez-faire capitalism with an ideological commitment to the individual: profit with personality, so to speak. If we accept that capitalism breeds high levels of repression and that individualism yields a "numbing encasement" bound up with an intense privatization of meaning, it follows that movements of liberation aimed at freeing the individual unwittingly reinforce precisely what they seek to dismantle. This is because such movements are committed to the self: its identity, personality, and idiosyncracies. Yet it is precisely the self, the discontinuous being, whose existence precludes a sense of closure and plenitude; in its submission to *logos*, it denies the dialectic between being and nonbeing. Movements of liberation seek to restore the individual's wholeness and unity, to provide it with a certain truth and authenticity to which it is entitled. The individual's acclimation to the reality principle, however, ensures that repression has been internalized, that it has accepted the fiction of personality that must be rethought in order for repression to be lessened. Thus liberationist movements frequently search the discontinuous realm for something that is in fact continuous. Hence those who affirm the individual fail to see beyond its differentiated apprehension of reality; in this, their quest is misguided. They deny the maternal, the abject, which alone responds to the primal urge for continuity. Were sexual repression truly lessened in our culture—lessened through a reorganization of our culture and its ethos, not a righting of history's wrongs—the erotic realm would no longer be such a contested, disputed terrain, forever in need of analysis, defence, and proclamation. Rather, it would be integrated into humanity in what Marcuse terms a "mature" way. It would be an impulse having numerous expressions through a body no longer conceived as a mere instrument of labor.

Might obscenity signal a longing to resolve the conflict between human need and ideological commitment, to proclaim from the beyond even within the confines of culture? I believe this to be the case. This is the theoretical framework in which I situate the topic of obscenity within the contemporary United States. Of course, the issue is rendered more complex by the actual politics of the debates surrounding it. For if the obscene always highlights the provisional nature of the reality principle, surely there are those who wish to monitor jealously those who can draw attention to this fact. To announce the tenuousness of culture's laws is to announce the possibility of change, the rewriting of those laws, the reshuffling of the power relations that currently inhere between hegemon and other. Naturally, then, the hegemon has an interest in controlling who can tamper with the organization of culture, who can challenge its limits. I examine these issues in the last chapter.

CHAPTER FIVE

Obscenity and American Culture: Control

Who controls the reality principle, the boundaries separating civilization from the abject realm devoid of taboo? Who decides how and when we transgress this principle, thereby revealing its provisional nature and mocking its putative hold on civilization? Such questions of course allude to the highly political nature of the obscenity debates, for negotiating the divide between civilization and the contrapuntal is always, on some level, about power, authority, and the ability to name. Yet these more immediate political concerns are never divorced from deeper theoretical issues. Who controls obscenity can never be separated from the question of what it is and how it operates. Hence if analyzed deeply, pornography, Robert Mapplethorpe, 2 Live Crew, and so forth reveal how all obscene expression[1] calls into question the impact and cogency of cultural mandates.

If controversial artistic expression always challenges the limits of culture, are there reasons why, at this moment in time, obscenity seems to represent a particularly charged issue on the American cultural and political scene? Is there something about contemporary America that is particularly threatened by the dialectic between being and nonbeing, by an awareness of reality's somewhat fictitious, provisional nature? I believe this to be the case. Specifically, I believe that the increasing loss of our status as world hegemon contributes to the need of certain groups to reconfirm our position, to reassert the interests of white mainstream America. These groups, often of a conservative stripe, insist that America remains the world's leading nation, and that it does so because of a certain moral rectitude. Conversely, other groups take a different view of the current American social, political, and economic scene. Important for our purposes is the fact that these groups, generally less conservative, insist upon the heterogeneous, multiracial, multicultural fabric of American society and are more willing to accept this country's slippage from its formerly hegemonic position. Let us examine these two points—America's heterogeneity and its decline as a leading power—separately.

The Postmodernism of American Culture

The United States is an ethnically and culturally diverse nation whose demographics are changing. Socially and culturally, the presence of others is increasingly felt in this country. Most striking is the rate at which the African-American, Asian-American, and especially Hispanic populations are growing. In time, these groups' interests and influence are bound to outstrip and outweigh those of mainstream Americans, at least in the country's urban areas. While recent appointments made by the Clinton administration garner them political power and visibility, they are also culturally prominent: Toni Morrison, Alice Walker, Amy Tan, and Maxine Hong Kingston are counted among our most celebrated authors; Spike Lee is a world-famous film director; and rap, hip-hop, and Hispanic music are becoming increasingly popular. Added to such ethnic considerations is, of course, the changing role of women, which has greatly altered both the public and private spheres of American life. Hence the Anita Hill, William Kennedy Smith, Murphy Brown, and Rodney King incidents—"can't we all just get along?"—have captured the attention of the American public, as have the ongoing feuds over reproductive rights, family values, and NEA funding. Despite the rhetoric and policies aimed at safeguarding hegemonic control, then, the American status quo—white, middle class, of European descent—clearly stands threatened; if nothing else, sheer demographics and the changing status of women point to this fact. Any effort to unequivocally promote an ethos reminiscent of former times, to suggest that a solid core of middle America stands firm, will founder on this count.

Witness the recent discussion over family values. This discussion began with criticisms registered against women who willingly bring a child into the world without a live-in father. Implicit in these criticisms is the statement that the nuclear family is integral to American culture, that being American is not entirely compatible with choosing a lifestyle outside the parameters of the traditional family. I would counter this statement with two observations: First, statistical evidence demonstrates that only one-third of contemporary American families conform to the nuclear prototype. There are simply too many divorces and out-of-wedlock births to allow that model to be called the norm. Second and of particular importance is the fact that African-American families have long counted women as their head of household. As far back as 1965, the Moynihan Report, commissioned by President Johnson as part of his "war on poverty," noted that African-American families were typically headed by a woman, that the roles of husband and wife were "reversed."[2] Such statistics prompted the report to wrongly label African-American family life "a tangle of pathology." Hence although the traditional nuclear family may describe an American tradition, or even a culturally desired goal, it simply does not constitute the norm in contemporary American life. The fabric of this culture has changed with the increase in the number of working women and the rise in the African-American population; moreover, the rate at which the Asian-American and especially Hispanic populations are rising ensures that this fabric will continue to change.

What then does it mean to be American, to be part of a nation so committed to pluralism, so characterized by heterogeneity with all its good and bad melting pot attributes, so lacking in any fixed cultural matrix? Certainly it means to be enmeshed in tremendous change and a sense of relativism. In America, the lexicon of cultural signifiers is especially open to interpretation. Social norms, mores, and opinions thus yield to private interpretation and an individualistic ethos. American culture truly accommodates the individual; any American who visits a foreign country recognizes its inhabitants' attention to cultural norms and mores as contrasted with American individualism. Hence upon visiting New York, Julia Kristeva commented that she found American culture to be very "postmodern": Here, things are fluid, open-ended, lacking in any overarching cultural matrix that might render meaning less private. In a sense, then, this nation has always been characterized by an absence of metanarrative, an absence that Jean-François Lyotard claims typifies postmodernity.[3] Perhaps more than anywhere else, multiculturalism and cultural relativism announce their presence in the United States; they are sometimes heavy and imposing, but always important. They typify American life. I believe that the multiculturalism, fluidity, and conflict inherent in our culture, along with our slippage as the leading power, contributes to a marked sense of ambiguity in American society. One might argue that we are now more postmodern than ever.

I believe that, on one level, we would like to replace the postmodern with something consensual, public, and shared. For political conservatives, this means rehabilitating traditional values in hope of garnering stability; for liberals, it means reasserting the role of government in negotiating more collectivist policies. There is consensus, then, among different groups of people as to what their desired administration should do. Yet the larger question of what it means to be an American results in anything but closure. An illustration: Spike Lee's *Do The Right Thing* deliberately avoids offering a clear, succinct prescription for what it means to "stay Black," a mandate that is nevertheless uttered to the protagonist, Mookie, on several occasions. Still, the film rightly insists that African-Americans need not simply assimilate into mainstream American culture. This message resonates against the backdrop of Mookie's ethnically diverse neighborhood. Aside from Blacks, it consists mostly of Hispanics and Koreans, all of whom bear no dearth of racial and ethnic grudges. For instance, in one scene, various characters do nothing but utter a battery of ugly epithets against targeted groups—African-Americans, Jews, Hispanics, Koreans, Italian-Americans—while the camera zooms in on their angry faces. Is it any wonder that Mookie knows the experience of being other but not what it means to "stay" that way?

As mentioned, the ability of diverse ethnic groups to challenge the limits of American culture is enhanced by our changing status as a world power. America is not reconfirming its position as hegemonic ruler in the world arena but is experiencing tremendous vulnerability internationally and domestically. We no longer lead as an industrial nation: We are ranked fifth in the world. Thwarted by economic competitors, we lag behind the Japanese and fear German reunification as well as European integration. At this writing, our economy is in a recession; we are experiencing very slow economic growth, one deficient in job creation, and our wages are no longer the highest in the world. Certain indicators of our standard of living, such as secondary education and health care, are deplorably disorganized and deficient when placed alongside their counterparts in other advanced industrial nations. Since Vietnam, we cannot say that we win every war, and our presence abroad is frequently perceived as imperialist and meddlesome. Moreover, the international dynamic is now greatly altered given the end of the Cold War, German reunification, the disintegration of the Soviet Union, collapse of the Soviet bloc, and European integration.

Although the state of being in flux is something many industrial nations are experiencing, only the United States is undergoing a retreat from our former status as world leader. Hence the very need to employ a rhetoric of hegemonic control, so pronounced in certain areas of American politics, bespeaks an underlying awareness of this country's increasing vulnerability, its fluxuating international status, its conflictedness and consequent sense of self-ambiguity. I believe that such ambiguity and conflictedness render obscenity a particularly charged issue in our culture. America may well be unique among nations, and may claim that particular brand of innovation, vitality, and free-spiritedness associated with it. But we no longer stand as hegemon in the world arena. With our hegemony thus undermined, I believe that perhaps more than other nations we subliminally feel the consensual limits of our culture to be under renegotiation. Our ideological boundaries are in flux. The enterprise of remapping and redefining these boundaries, begun in the sixties, assumes new and different guises.

One such guise is to deny our changing and declining status, to insist that we remain at the helm. This denial occurs despite the fact that we are rivaled if not overshadowed by other nations; it occurs despite our fractious politics at home. One specific form this denial takes is that of redoubling the efforts of mainstream America in asserting control over our cultural ethos, in defining in black-and-white terms what constitutes American society and how that society should operate. Hence our nation's others—African-Americans, Hispanics, Asian-Americans, Jews, lesbians and gays, and of course women—are, by some, codified as increasingly subversive. Our shifting position gives special play to their contrapuntal dimension, for such groups typically do not fit an agenda supposedly geared toward traditional values. In their otherness, such groups are targeted as embodying dangerous forces, operating against the interests of the status quo, and challenging the limits of American culture. How threatening, then, is their overt expression of the obscene; how in need of containment their unabashed efforts to proclaim from the beyond. Efforts to label certain works obscene reveal the need in American culture to disempower such marginalized groups from exerting control over the reality principle, from threatening to undermine or displace the limits of culture. Presumably, they are not sufficiently privileged to be able to play with the boundaries separating civilization from the abject, from dedifferentiation. They cannot contemplate this realm directly via sexually explicit material, or via references to scatology or eschatology, for these call into question the distinction between the reality principle and the oppositional realm of the maternal, of continuity. Negotiating the reality principle by referring to abjection represents too charged an issue, it seems, for just anyone to handle. Obviously, then, debates over obscenity in the arts touch upon more than questions of decency and sexual standards. They are red herrings; obscenity delves much deeper, going "right up into the ass of death," forcing us to face the negotiability, the tenuousness of the reality principle.

Thus when the reality principle, the established limits of culture, are under renegotiation, there exists a special kind of tension and volatility surrounding the category of the obscene. This is especially true given the backdrop of a culture in which meaning is already so privatized, so tailored to the individual. The absence of an overarching cultural matrix renders the topic particularly fractious. Taken together, I believe these hallmarks of contemporary American culture help explain why debates about obscenity promise to endure, to remain highly political and largely unresolved.

Does this suggest that cultures that are less in flux, for whom meaning is less privatized and who admit continuity are more at ease with this category's presence? Given their own stability, are such cultures more comfortable with obscenity's ability to challenge its limits, to highlight its provisional quality? My answer is in part speculative, because I have lived all of my adult life in the United States in the wake of the sixties. Still, I believe that to some extent such questions can be answered in the affirmative. Where there is consensus and stability, a subliminal recognition of our need for continuity and of reality's fictional nature, obscenity is a less charged issue, a less threatening category. Expressions of the obscene are less feared in cultures that uphold the distinction between consensual reality and the dionysian realm of dedifferentiation; such cultures, it would seem, can support the dialectic between being and nonbeing, as they sustain the tension between the life and death impulses. Questions of continuity do not seek resolution in the discontinuous realm, and the obscene is not forced to submit to *logos*. Rather, a shared sense of reality, nevertheless recognized as provisional, seemingly attenuates the isolation, the numbing encasement, that our culture breeds.

Cloud 9: Victorian Promiscuity, Contemporary Pathos

Caryl Churchill's lively two-act play, *Cloud 9*, helps clarify my point.[4] The play's first act is set in British colonial Africa circa 1880, and focuses on the life of an English family upholding the crown's imperialist mission. Envoys of English culture, eight of the nine characters are white and execute the "white man's burden." They seek to tame the literal and metaphorical wilds of Africa— the African people, African culture, the human id—while striving to convert its natives to a British, Christian, explicitly Victorian way of life. Although British, Victorian culture may not be universally superlative, in their minds it unquestionably overshadows the life they observe on "the dark continent." Indeed, it is their allegiance to the crown that primarily endows these characters with their personal identities. They understand themselves essentially as British subjects. They have a common bond, a shared sense of self. Hence, for *Cloud 9*'s first-act characters, meaning is not privatized. No one interprets the world individually, tailoring it to his or her idiosyncrasies. Included in their vocabularies are such words as "mission," "duty," "empire," and "sin." No one claims a privately forged identity, and certainly not a "sexual identity." On the contrary, the characters strive to live up to the world's expectations of them as English subjects and to dutifully execute their responsibilities.

Moreover, with this exploration of Victorian family life, Churchill seems intent on illustrating the Foucaultian enterprise of discrediting the repressive hypothesis. In her rendition of nineteenth-century mores, sexual silence and prohibitions do anything but curtail sexual activity. *Cloud 9*'s first act brims with sexual encounters, all of which transgress the prevailing ethos sanctioning only monogamous, heterosexual marriage. This act illustrates how the prevalence of firm boundaries allows the characters to enjoy "an erotic sense of reality." Revealed to us is an abundance of comic sexual adventure in an age remembered for its restraint, discretion, and sexual silence. The characters chase one another across the stage, disappear under skirts, enjoy stolen moments together, sneak away for an illicit tryst. Publically, they defend the family, marriage, and monogamy; privately, there is no dearth of adulterous liaisons, gay, lesbian, and cross-generational activity, deceit, betrayal, and conscious transgression of boundaries. The following exchange takes place between Harry and nine-year-old Edward:

> Edward: You know what we did when you were here before. I want to do it again. I try to do it to myself but it's not as good. Don't you want to anymore?
> Harry: I do, but it's a sin and a crime and it's also wrong.
> Edward: But we'll do it anyway won't we?
> Harry: Yes of course.[5]

Nearly every character holds some surprise in store for the audience. While they never discuss sexuality, nor indeed their sexual "identities," they perform sexual acts with abandon.

The play's second act takes place one hundred years later. Set in London, it revolves around many of the same characters from Act One who, despite the time interval, have aged only twenty-five years. These characters have abandoned the white man's burden in Africa and have come back to England, no longer an aggressive world power. Situating the same set of characters in two different time periods allows Churchill to contrast the rigid, prohibition-laden sensibilities of Victorian British colonizers against their freewheeling modern-day counterparts, thereby scrutinizing the themes of sexual liberation and identity. Indeed, the play juxtaposes the sexual silence and secrecy characteristic of Victorian propriety as distinct from the promiscuity, garrulousness, and concern with sexual identity that typify contemporary culture. This juxtaposition is what lends the piece its critical distance, its dramatic effectiveness, and its humor.

By the second act, sex has undergone an enormous transformation. The sexual revolution has left its imprint. Civilization's taboos have presumably been rethought, and the reality principle renegotiated. The characters have therefore reoriented their "sexual identities" in which they now so firmly believe and have brought a new set of private meanings to bear on the topic of sex, meanings that didn't exist in the first act. Indeed, with the putative liberation comes an increased focus on identity, for the former cultural matrix from which characters took their bearings—a matrix upheld by the pillars of religion, the crown, the family, monogamy, and heterosexuality—no longer prevails. As a nation, England's identity is under renegotiation; Victorian stability is supplanted by a state of flux and indeterminacy. For this and other reasons, the characters do not understand themselves primarily as British subjects. They are liberated women and men, lesbians and gays; nearly all are economically independent persons making their way outside of a traditional family structure. The absence of a cultural matrix thus leaves them burdened with the responsibility of forging a private identity, of bringing meaning to their highly individualized existences.

Throughout its four scenes, we watch the characters struggle through their intensely private battles without guidelines or traditional paradigms to fall back on. It is not only life plans that the characters grapple with, however. Relationships, jobs, money, security: Although these things greatly concern Churchill's second-act characters, what troubles them most deeply are their private identities, especially their sexual identities, to which they look for closure, fulfillment, and completion. Indeed, sexual identity and the promise this holds constitutes a central theme in *Cloud 9*'s second act, a theme sharply contrasting with the first act's emphasis on an overarching social order wherein privatized sexual identities were undermined and even denied. By contrast, Act Two presents us with contemporary Londoners firmly committed to sexual freedom and in search of sexual fulfillment. We know this, because they speak so openly and consistently about their sexual exploits, frustrations, and desires. They believe in *talking* about sex. Hence, as observed by Foucault, we witness a true proliferation of discourse surrounding the topic of sex, sensing the characters' conviction that the ability to talk openly about the matter signals some advancement along the way toward completion, closure, "the big O." Act Two is characterized by

> a discourse in which sex, the revelation of truth, the overturning of global laws, the proclamation of a new day to come, and the promise of a certain felicity are linked together. Today it is sex that serves as a support for the ancient form—so familiar and important in the West—of preaching. A great sexual sermon . . . has swept through our societies over the last decades; it has chastised the old order, denounced hypocrisy, and praised the rights of the immediate and the real; it has made people dream of a New City. The Franciscans are called to mind.[6]

And yet sex doesn't deliver. Despite the hue and cry about liberated, "true" identities, hardly anyone in the second act seems happy. Everyone is angry, confused, sad, and in turmoil. Victoria leaves her husband Martin for a woman named Lin. Betty has left

Clive, and has difficulty adjusting to life on her own (Betty: "I'll never be able to manage. If I can't even walk down the street by myself."[7]). The gay couple, Gerry and Edward, break up because Gerry needs more freedom. Later, he regrets this decision (Gerry: "There's never any trouble finding someone. I can have sex anytime. . . . I wake up at four o'clock sometimes. Birds. Silence. If I bring somebody home I never let them stay the night. Edward! Edward!"[8]) and asks Edward to come back. Sexuality, so pronounced a theme in the play's second act, is forever accompanied by anguish and despair. The characters seek constantly to reinterpret their sexual identities; they look for closure, fulfillment, orgasm; they hold fast to the promise of the repressive hypothesis stating that once taboo has been renegotiated, the erotic drive will breathe freely at last.

And yet, throughout the entire second act, sexuality appears as a most troubled dimension of the characters' lives, one marked by anguish, despair, and frustration. It brings them anything but fulfillment; in keeping with Foucault's observations, the proliferation of discourse succeeds only in keeping them worried about their erotic identities and performances. Where sexuality is concerned, they feel shortchanged. What are they doing wrong? Frustration is evident in the angry words that Martin delivers to Victoria shortly before they separate:

> Martin: What it is about sex, when we talk while it's happening I get to feel like it's a driving lesson. Left, right, a little faster, carry on, slow down. . . . So I lost my erection last night not because I'm not prepared to talk, it's just that taking in technical information is in a different part of the brain and also I don't like to feel you do it better to yourself. I have read the Hite report. I do know that women have to learn to get their pleasure despite our clumsy attempts at expressing undying devotion and ecstasy. . . . My one aim is to give you pleasure. My one aim is to give you rolling orgasms like I do other women. So why the hell don't you have them?[9]

Whereas the play's first act was funny, its second evokes pathos.

Churchill's *Cloud 9* presents us with two cultures in which taboo, prohibition, and repression play strikingly different roles. The first act finds these concepts and hence the obscene solidly established. The second studies their reconsideration; they are now utterly relative categories upon which individuals decide for themselves. The privatized meaning experienced by the second-act characters thus owes itself to the provisional reality principle, destabilized by a now-negotiable set of social taboos. Each character chooses privately which boundaries to cross, what constitutes transgression, how to proclaim from the beyond. The cultural lexicon has been disrupted—what means what anymore?—such that the characters are essentially left to their private understandings. A longing for continuity now seeks resolution in the discontinuous realm.

Most salient is the fact that the state of flux in which the second-act characters find themselves enmeshed proves so overwhelming that the very existence of the beyond, of continuity, appears questionable. How can a sense of continuity, mergence, and union be achieved when the very category of continuity stands under renegotiation? How can the innate longing for an unmediated relationship to the world posited in the death drive be satiated when sexuality now corresponds singularly to human identity, the discontinuous realm, the fiction of personality? When sexuality resonates with taboo, prohibition, even sin, it invokes something primal, something that bypasses the individual. However, when in its reconceptualization it answers to the differentiated realm of the individual, it no longer resonates with the basic human drives but becomes subsumed under the individuated realm of identity. It has been appropriated by discontinuity, by the reality principle, and forced to submit to *logos*.

I would argue that cultures that clearly recognize the boundaries of transgression uphold the obscene, thereby providing a relationship between the individual and continuity, the individual and his or her death drive. On the other hand, cultures that cast this issue within the differentiated realm of the rational, acclimated individual reorient this relationship, bringing unbearable expectation to the realm of identity, personality, and privatized meaning. I believe that contemporary America breeds such a culture, one wherein continuity seeks resolution in the discontinuous realm.

No Simple Antidote

Such pronouncements should not be interpreted as prescribing a cure for the problem they describe. I am in no way suggesting that we return to Victorianism and abandon all forms of identity politics, movements of liberation, and concerns with the self. Although I view as problematic the fact that contemporary society does not uphold the obscene, but relegates it to the discontinuous realm, I have no remedy, no simple antidote to this situation. Indeed, this cultural disposition, one that breeds "numbing encasements," strikes me as part and parcel of our social and political profile. It emanates from our commitment to individualism and free enterprise, our investment in rationality and empiricism, our indebtedness to secular humanism and the Enlightenment. The political, economic, and social fabric of our society may ultimately change, but for now our investment in discontinuity remains deeply ingrained in the traditions, ethos, and habits that make us American.

What can more readily and easily change, however, is our understanding of what obscenity is and of the function it serves. It serves to clarify how civilization's hold on the human subject remains tenuous and negotiable; it forever reminds us of how forcefully the irrational pleasure principle weighs upon human impulse. Our culture's investment in the masculine reality principle thus guards against the engulfing counterforce of the feminine. Although a heightened intellectual appreciation of the obscene is undoubtedly useful, still I insist that the relationship between continuity and discontinuity—the phallic reality principle and its obscene feminine counterpoint—must be renegotiated at the social and economic level. However meaningful our apprehension of the obscene, any renegotiation of this category must be undertaken collectively and materially rather than individually.

Will feminism reorient the gender archetypes so integral to our culture and crucial to this investigation? Will the changing role of women, the growing number of single-parent households, increased male participation in childrearing, and cultural tolerance of alternative lifestyles erode the current bipolarity between a feminine pleasure principle and a masculine reality principle?[10] Certainly such questions, which probe the relationship between empirical and psychic reality, have already been amply discussed in feminist circles, particularly by those arguing for changed family structures and shared parenting. I see no reason to doubt that radically altered structures and relations might not seriously impact their psychic and metaphorical counterparts. If public and private, transcendent and immanent, masculine and feminine are indeed cultural constructs, there is no reason to deny their mutability. At this moment, however, I believe the metaphorical feminine to be cast as the envoy of otherness, imbued with contrapuntal status. Naming this status contrapuntal, we have seen, does not represent a disparaging gesture, but one that acknowledges the feminine's subversive, creative power.

This returns us to the female body, and to certain feminist readings of pornography. These readings set women apart from other marginalized groups and shed tremendous light on the category of the obscene. Women are particularly charged with otherness, for female bodily parts, the Medusa-like genitals, directly invoke the abject realm of the maternal, the outside-of-meaning. In its "enemy" status, the female body proclaims that the reality principle is negotiable. It signals the possibility of transgressing our discrete identities and of being joined to the continuous realm. I believe that American culture especially longs for what is "enemy" and contrapuntal. Hence in this country, a woman's body represents a particularly contested terrain, its political divisiveness and emotional weight woven into the very fabric of American society.

Notes

Introduction

1. See Hester Eisenstein, *Contemporary Feminist Thought* (Boston: G. K. Hall, 1983).

2. Quoted in *Caught Looking: Feminism, Pornography and Censorship*, Kate Ellis, Beth Jaker, Nan D. Hunter, Barbara O'Dair, and Abby Tallmer, eds. (Seattle: Real Comet Press, 1988), 26.

3. The term "archeplot," used in a discussion about pornography and gender relations, is credited to Susanne Kappeler. See her *The Pornography of Representation* (Minneapolis: University of Minnesota Press, 1986).

4. See Kappeler, *Pornography of Representation*, and Annette Kuhn, *The Power of the Image: Essays on Representation and Sexuality* (Boston: Routledge & Kegan Paul, 1985).

5. As examples of these different positions, see Alexander Downs, *The New Politics of Pornography* (Chicago: University of Chicago Press, 1989); Andrea Dworkin, *Pornography: Men Possessing Women* (New York: Perigree Books, 1981); Catharine MacKinnon, *Feminism Unmodified: Discourses on Life and Law* (Cambridge: Harvard University Press, 1987); *Caught Looking: Feminism, Pornography and Censorship*, Kate Ellis, Beth Jaker, Nan D. Hunter, Barbara O'Dair, and Abby Tallmer, eds.; Alan Soble, *Pornography: Marxism, Feminism, and the Future of Sexuality* (New Haven: Yale University Press, 1986); and Linda Williams, *Hard Core: Power, Pleasure, and the "Frenzy of the Visible"* (Berkeley: University of California Press, 1989).

6. "Obscenity" is the legal term for unprotected speech, the definition of which I discuss presently. Let me make clear from the start, however, that much pornography is not "obscene."

7. See *Art News* (November 1989, December 1990); *Art in America* (May 1990, December 1990).

8. See *Art in America* (May 1990): 41.

9. See especially Douglas Davis' "Art and Contradiction: Helms, Censorship, and the Serpent" in *Art in America* (May 1990): 55–61.

10. I am indebted to Cynthia Witman for the phrase "subconsciously consensual limits."

11. This idea comes from Norman O. Brown's *Life Against Death: The Psychoanalytic Meaning of History* (Middletown, Conn.: Wesleyan University Press, 1985).

12. See Georges Bataille, *Erotism: Death and Sensuality* (San Francisco: City Lights Books, 1986); Jessica Benjamin, *The Bonds of Love: Psychoanalysis, Feminism, and the Problem of Domination* (New York: Pantheon Books, 1988); Susan Sontag, "The Pornographic Imagination," in *A Susan Sontag Reader* (New York: Farrar, Straus & Giroux, 1982), 205–33.

13. See Stephen Holden, "Madonna Re-Creates Herself—Again," *The New York Times* (March 19, 1989), 12.

14. Pauline Réage, *The Story of O* (New York: Ballantine Books, 1984), 39, 76.

15. Joel Kovel, "The Antidialectic of Pornography," in *Men Confront Pornography*, Michael S. Kimmel, ed. (New York: Crown Publishers, 1990), 153–67.

16. Kovel, "The Antidialectic of Pornography," 156.

17. Kovel, "The Antidialectic of Pornography," 155.

18. Max Horkheimer and Theodor Adorno, *The Dialectic of Enlightenment* (New York: Continuum Press, 1972), 3, 5.

19. Jessica Benjamin, "Master and Slave: The Fantasy of Erotic Domination," in *Powers of Desire: The Politics of Sexuality*, Ann Snitow, Christine Stansell, and Sharon Thompson, eds. (New York: Monthly Review Press, 1983), 296.

20. See Christopher Lasch's "Introduction" to Brown's *Life Against Death*, vii–xiii.

21. I develop this theme in Chapter Four, in which I discuss Herbert Marcuse's reading of Freudian drive theory.

22. Michel Foucault, *The History of Sexuality, Volume I* (New York: Vintage Books, 1980), 5.

Chapter One

1. See Dworkin, *Pornography: Men Possessing Women*; Susanne Kappeler, *Pornography of Representation*; Catharine MacKinnon, *Feminism Unmodified*.

2. I am indebted to Kevin McDonnell for these terms.

3. Catharine MacKinnon, "Not A Moral Issue," in *Feminism Unmodified*, 148.

4. MacKinnon, "Not A Moral Issue," 148.

5. Dworkin, *Pornography: Men Possessing Women*, 110–11.

6. Kuhn, *Power of the Image*, 31.

7. Kappeler, *Pornography of Representation*, 104.

8. Kappeler, *Pornography of Representation*, 136.

9. John Berger, *Ways of Seeing* (London: British Broadcasting Corporation, 1986) 46–47.

10. Berger, *Ways of Seeing*, 55.

11. See Helen Longino's "Pornography, Oppression, and Freedom: A Closer Look," in *Take Back the Night*, Laura Lederer, ed. (New York: William Morrow, 1980), 40–54.

12. Soble, *Pornography*, 57.

13. Kuhn, *Power of the Image*, 39.

14. I believe this juxtaposition to be correct, but let me not ignore those troubling moments in the film when Paul is abusive to Jeanne. For instance, in one scene he rapes her.

15. Kuhn, *Power of the Image*, 40.

16. For a detailed account of these events, see especially Downs, *New Politics of Pornography*.

17. See Downs, *New Politics of Pornography*, 43–50. See also Jeanne Barkey, "Minneapolis Porn Ordinance," in *off our backs* (January 1984): 1–3.

18. Susan Griffin, "Pornography and Silence," in *Made from This Earth: An Anthology of Writings by Susan Griffin* (New York: Harper & Row, 1982), 144.

19. Edward Said, *Orientalism* (New York: Vintage Books, 1979).

20. Said, *Orientalism*, 38–39.

21. Said, *Orientalism*, 45.

22. Virginia Woolf, *A Room of One's Own* (San Diego: Harcourt Brace Jovanovich, 1990), 35.

23. Simone de Beauvoir, *The Second Sex* (New York: Vintage Books, 1974).

24. Dorothy Dinnerstein, *The Mermaid and the Minotaur: Sexual Arrangements and Human Malaise* (New York: Harper & Row, 1977).

25. De Beauvoir, *Second Sex*, 187.

26. De Beauvoir, *Second Sex*, 187.

27. Griffin, "Pornography and Silence," 121, 129.

28. Dinnerstein, *Mermaid and the Minotaur*, 5.

29. Kuhn, *Power of the Image*, 35, 46.

30. Kovel, "The Antidialectic of Pornography," 165. In their writings and through conversations, Susan Buck-Morss and Kathleen Jones also helped me appreciate the failure of pornography.

Chapter Two

1. See especially his *Civilization and Its Discontents*, James Strachey, ed. (New York: W. W. Norton, 1989).

2.   Freud, *Civilization and Its Discontents*, 25.

3.   Compare, for instance, Kate Millett's *Sexual Politics* (New York: Ballantine Books, 1987) with Juliette Mitchell's *Psychoanalysis and Feminism* (New York: Pantheon Books, 1974).

4.   In this vein, see Sarah Kofman's witty and insightful *The Enigma of Woman: Woman in Freud's Writing* (Ithaca: Cornell University Press, 1985).

5.   Daniel Stern challenges this assumption in his influential *The Interpersonal World of the Infant: A View from Psychoanalysis and Developmental Psychology* (New York: Basic Books, 1985).

6.   The term is problematic, for it implies much more consensus among feminist scholars employing Lacanian and deconstructive methods than actually exists.

7.   See Jessica Benjamin, *The Bonds of Love*; Nancy Chodorow, *The Reproduction of Mothering: Psychoanalysis and the Sociology of Gender* (Berkeley: University of California Press, 1978); Chodorow, *Feminism and Psychoanalytic Theory* (New Haven: Yale University Press, 1989); Dorothy Dinnerstein, *Mermaid and the Minotaur*; Carol Gilligan, *In A Different Voice: Psychological Theory and Women's Development* (Cambridge: Harvard University Press, 1982).

8.   In *Civilization and Its Discontents*, he writes: "I cannot discover this 'oceanic' feeling in myself. It is not easy to deal scientifically with feelings" (11).

9.   Freud, *Civilization and Its Discontents*, 15.

10.   For an excellent discussion of this topic, see Linda Zerilli's "Rememoration or War? French Feminist Narrative and the Politics of Self-Representation" in *differences: A Journal of Feminist Cultural Studies* 3 (Spring 1991): 1–19

11.   Freud, "Medusa's Head," in *Sigmund Freud: Collected Papers*, James Strachey, ed. (New York: Basic Books, Vol. 5, 1959), 105.

12.   Freud, "Fetishism," in *Collected Papers*, 201.

13.   See Edith Hamilton, *Mythology* (Boston: Little, Brown, and Company, 1942), 204.

14.   Quoted in Hamilton, *Mythology*, 201.

15.   Freud, "Medusa's Head," 105.

16.   Freud, "Medusa's Head," 105.

17.   Freud, *Civilization and Its Discontents*, 59.

18.   Freud, "Medusa's Head," 106.

19.   It should be mentioned that this dichotomy between the pre-oedipal mother and the oedipal father has been criticized as too simplistic. For instance, Benjamin insists that classical psychoanalysis obscures the psychic presence of an irrational, archaic father and of a rational, progressive mother due to its reliance on splitting. See her *Bonds of Love*, chapter 4.

20.   Dinnerstein, *Mermaid and the Minotaur*, 66.

21.   See for instance her "Some Thoughts on the Ego Ideal," *Psycho-*

analytic Quarterly 45 (1976): 349–60; *The Ego Ideal: A Psychoanalytic Essay on the Malady of the Ideal* (New York: W. W. Norton, 1985).

22. Freud, *Civilization and Its Discontents*, 20.

23. Herbert Marcuse, *Eros and Civilization: A Philosophical Inquiry into Freud* (Boston: Beacon Press, 1974), 67.

24. See her *The Bonds of Love*, chapter 4.

25. Julia Kristeva, "Stabat Mater," in *The Kristeva Reader*, Toril Moi, ed. (New York: Columbia University Press, 1986), 179–80.

26. Timothy Beneke, "Intrusive Images and Subjectified Bodies: Notes on Visual Heterosexual Porn," in *Men Confront Pornography*, 168–87.

27. Beneke, "Intrusive Images and Subjectified Bodies," 174.

28. Beneke, "Intrusive Images and Subjectified Bodies," 171.

29. Beneke, "Intrusive Images and Subjectified Bodies," 172.

30. Niccolo Machiavelli, *The Prince*, Robert M. Adams, ed. (New York: W. W. Norton, 1992), 21.

Chapter Three

1. Sigmund Freud, *Beyond the Pleasure Principle*, translated by James Strachey (New York: W. W. Norton, 1961), 33.

2. Freud, *Beyond the Pleasure Principle*, 32.

3. This term is borrowed from Jessica Benjamin's "Master and Slave," 282.

4. Kristeva, "Revolution in Poetic Langauge," in *The Kristeva Reader*, 95.

5. Julia Kristeva, *Powers of Horror: An Essay on Abjection* (New York: Columbia University Press, 1982), 1, 3–4.

6. Joyce Rebeta-Burditt, *The Cracker Factory* (New York: Macmillan, 1977), 174.

7. Rebeta-Burditt, *The Cracker Factory*, 173–4.

8. Sontag, "The Pornographic Imagination," 221.

9. Bataille, *Erotism: Death and Sensuality*, 17, 31.

10. Evelyn Waugh, *Brideshead Revisited: The Sacred and Profane Memoirs of Captain Charles Ryder* (Boston: Little, Brown, and Company, 1945), 169.

11. Waugh, *Brideshead Revisited*, 169.

12. Waugh, *Brideshead Revisited*, 5.

13. Waugh, *Brideshead Revisited*, 351.

14. Brown, *Life Against Death*, 93.

15. Domna Stanton, "Difference on Trial: A Critique of the Maternal Metaphor in Cixous, Irigaray, and Kristeva," in *The Poetics of Gender*, Nancy K. Miller, ed. (New York: Columbia University Press, 1986), 158.

16.   Jacques Derrida, *Spurs: Nietzsche's Styles*, translated by Barbara Harlow (Chicago: University of Chicago Press, 1979), 51, 55.

17.   Kristeva, *Powers of Horror*, 15, 22.

18.   Kristeva, *Powers of Horror*, 23–24.

19.   Elizabeth Grosz, *Sexual Subversions: Three French Feminists* (Sydney: Allen and Unwin, 1990), 74.

Chapter Four

1.   Karl Marx, "Estranged Labour," in *The Marx-Engels Reader*, Robert Tucker, ed. (second edition; New York: W. W. Norton, 1978), 74–75.

2.   Karl Marx and Friedrich Engels, "The German Ideology: Part I," in *The Marx-Engels Reader*, 160.

3.   Brown, *Life Against Death*, 84. Chapter seven of this book discusses the concept of instinctual dialectics in depth.

4.   Marcuse, *Eros and Civilization*, 155.

5.   Brown, *Life Against Death*, 84–85.

6.   Marcuse, *Eros and Civilization*, 199, 208.

7.   Marcuse, *Eros and Civilization*, 161.

8.   Marcuse, *Eros and Civilization*, 162.

9.   Marcuse, *Eros and Civilization*, 161.

10.   Marcuse, *Eros and Civilization*, 161.

11.   Quoted in Marcuse, *Eros and Civilization*, 153.

12.   Brown, *Love's Body* (New York: Random House, 1966), 215.

13.   Brown, *Love's Body*, 159.

14.   Brown, *Love's Body*, 266.

15.   Brown, *Love's Body*, 38.

16.   Brown, *Love's Body*, 221–22.

17.   Juliet Schor, *The Overworked American: The Unexpected Decline of Leisure* (New York: Basic Books, 1991).

18.   Benjamin, "Master and Slave," 282, 296. On this count, see also the work of Naomi Goldenberg.

19.   Susan Buck-Morss helped me arrive at this insight.

20.   Phelan, *Identity Politics*, 156.

21.   Brown, *Love's Body*, 15.

22.   Quoted in "Carnal Knowledge: Three Words to Avoid in Bed, and More from Dr. Ruth Westheimer," by Sally Lee, *Redbook* (September 1992): 66.

23.   Michel Foucault, *The History of Sexuality: Volume I* (New York: Vintage Books, 1980), 6.

24.   Foucault, *History of Sexuality*, 8–9.

Chapter Five

1. I use the phrase "obscene expression," yet recall my earlier caveat that not all forms of pornographic representation are deemed legally obscene.

2. *The Negro Family: The Case for National Action*, U.S. Department of Labor, Office Policy Planning and Research Staff (Greenwood, Conn.: Greenwood Press, 1981; reprint of 1965 edition).

3. Jean-François Lyotard, *The Postmodern Condition: A Report on Knowledge* (Minneapolis: University of Minnesota Press, 1989).

4. A collection of insightful essays on this play is contained in *Caryl Churchill: A Casebook*, Phyllis R. Randall, ed. (New York: Garland Publishing, 1988).

5. Caryl Churchill, *Cloud 9* (London: Pluto Press, 1983), 33–34.

6. Foucault, *History of Sexuality*, 7–8.

7. Churchill, 78.

8. Churchill, 99.

9. Churchill, 80–81.

10. See Chapter Two, footnote no. 18.

Select Bibliography

Art in America. May 1990.

Art in America. December 1990.

Art News. November 1989.

Barkey, Jeanne. "Minneapolis Porn Ordinance." *off our backs* (January 1984): 1–3.

Bataille, George. *Erotism: Death and Sensuality.* San Francisco: City Lights Books, 1986.

Beneke, Timothy. "Intrusive Images and Subjectified Bodies: Notes on Visual Heterosexual Porn." In *Men Confront Pornography*, edited by Michael S. Kimmel, 168–87. New York: Crown Publishers, 1990.

Benjamin, Jessica. *The Bonds of Love: Psychoanalysis, Feminism, and the Problem of Domination.* New York: Pantheon Books, 1988.

————. "Master and Slave: The Fantasy of Erotic Domination." In *Powers of Desire: The Politics of Sexuality*, edited by Ann Snitow, Christine Stansell, and Sharon Thompson, 280–99. New York: Monthly Review Press, 1983.

Berger, John. *Ways of Seeing.* London: British Broadcasting Corporation, 1986.

Brown, Norman O. *Life Against Death: The Psychoanalytic Meaning of History.* Middletown, Conn.: Wesleyan University Press, 1985.

———. *Love's Body*. New York: Random House, 1966.

Caryl Churchill: A Casebook. Edited by Phyllis Randall. New York: Garland Publishing, 1988.

Chasseguet-Smirgel, Janine. *The Ego Ideal: A Psychoanalytic Essay on the Malady of the Ideal*. New York: W. W. Norton, 1985.

———. "Some Thoughts on the Ego Ideal." *Psychoanalytic Quarterly* 45 (1976): 349–60.

Chodorow, Nancy. *Feminism and Psychoanalytic Theory*. New Haven: Yale University Press, 1989.

———. *The Reproduction of Mothering: Psychoanalysis and the Sociology of Gender*. Berkeley: University of California Press, 1978.

Churchill, Caryl. *Cloud 9*. London: Pluto Press, 1983.

Davis, Douglas. "Art and Contradiction: Helms, Censorship, and the Serpent." *Art in America* (May 1990, Vol. 78, 5): 55–61.

De Beauvoir, Simone. *The Second Sex*. New York: Vintage Books, 1974.

Derrida, Jacques. *Spurs: Nietzsche's Styles*. Translated by Barbara Harlow. Chicago: University of Chicago Press, 1979.

Dinnerstein, Dorothy. *The Mermaid and the Minotaur: Sexual Arrangements and Human Malaise*. New York: Harper & Row, 1977.

Downs, Alexander. *The New Politics of Pornography*. Chicago: University of Chicago Press, 1989.

Dworkin, Andrea. *Pornography: Men Possessing Women*. New York: Perigree Books, 1981.

Eisenstein, Hester. *Contemporary Feminist Thought*. Boston: G. K. Hall, 1983.

Ellis, Kate, Beth Jaker, Nan D. Hunter, Barbara O'Dair, and Abby Tallmer, eds. *Feminism, Pornography and Censorship*. Seattle: Real Comet Press, 1988.

Forster, E. M. *A Passage to India*. San Diego: Harcourt Brace Jovanovich, 1989.

Foucault, Michel. *The History of Sexuality, Volume I*. New York: Vintage Books, 1980.

Freud, Sigmund. *Beyond the Pleasure Principle*. Translated by James Strachey. New York: W. W. Norton, 1961.

―――. *Civilization and Its Discontents*. Edited by James Strachey. New York: W. W. Norton, 1989.

―――. "Fetishism," in *Sigmund Freud: Collected Papers*. Edited by James Strachey, 198–204. New York: Basic Books, 1959.

―――. "Medusa's Head," in *Sigmund Freud: Collected Papers*. Edited by James Strachey, 105–6. New York: Basic Books, 1959.

Gilligan, Carol. *In A Different Voice: Psychological Theory and Women's Development*. Cambridge: Harvard University Press, 1982.

Goldenberg, Naomi. *Changing of the Gods: Feminism and the End of Traditional Religions*. Boston: Beacon Press, 1979.

―――. *Returning Words to Flesh: Feminism, Psychoanalysis, and the Resurrection of the Body*. Boston: Beacon Press, 1990.

Griffin, Susan. "Pornography and Silence." In *Made from This Earth: An Anthology of Writings by Susan Griffin*, 110–60. New York: Harper & Row, 1982.

Grosz, Elizabeth. *Sexual Subversions: Three French Feminists*. Sydney: Allen and Unwin, 1990.

Hamilton, Edith. *Mythology*. Boston: Little, Brown, 1942.

Holden, Stephen. "Madonna Re-Creates Herself—Again." *The New York Times* (March 19, 1989): 1, 12.

Horkheimer, Max, and Theodor Adorno. *The Dialectic of Enlightenment*. New York: Continuum Press, 1972.

Kappeler, Susanne. *The Pornography of Representation*. Minneapolis: University of Minnesota Press, 1986.

Kofman, Sarah. *The Enigma of Woman: Woman in Freud's Writing*. Translated by Catherine Porter. Ithaca: Cornell University Press, 1985.

Kovel, Joel. "The Antidialectic of Pornography." In *Men Confront Pornography*, edited by Michael S. Kimmel, 153–67. New York: Crown Publishers, 1990.

Kristeva, Julia. "Revolution in Poetic Language." In *The Kristeva Reader*. Translated by Leon S. Roudiez. Edited by Toril Moi, 89–136. New York: Columbia University Press, 1986.

———. "Stabat Mater." In *The Kristeva Reader*. Translated by Leon S. Roudiez. Edited by Toril Moi, 160–86. New York: Columbia University Press, 1986.

———. *Powers of Horror: An Essay on Abjection*. Translated by Leon S. Roudiez. New York: Columbia University Press, 1982.

Kuhn, Annette. *The Power of the Image*. Boston: Routledge & Kegan Paul, 1985.

Lasch, Christopher. "Introduction." In Norman O. Brown's *Life Against Death: the Psychoanalytic Meaning of History*, vii–xiii. Middletown, Conn.: Wesleyan University Press, 1985.

Lee, Sally. "Carnal Knowledge: Three Words to Avoid in Bed." *Redbook* (September 1992): 64–66.

Longino, Helen. "Pornography, Oppression, and Freedom: A Closer Look." In *Take Back the Night*. Edited by Laura Lederer, 40–54. New York: William Morrow, 1980.

Lyotard, Jean-François. *The Postmodern Condition: A Report on Knowledge*. Minneapolis: University of Minnesota Press, 1989.

Machiavelli, Niccolo. *The Prince*. Translated and edited by Robert M. Adams. New York: W. W. Norton, 1992.

MacKinnon, Catharine. *Feminism Unmodified: Discourses on Life and Law*. Cambridge: Harvard University Press, 1987.

Marcuse, Herbert. *Eros and Civilization: A Philosophical Inquiry into Freud*. Boston: Beacon Press, 1974.

Marx, Karl. "Estranged Labour." In *The Marx-Engels Reader*, 2nd ed. Edited by Robert Tucker, 70–81. New York: W. W. Norton, 1978.

Marx, Karl, and Friedrich Engels. "The German Ideology: Part I." In *The Marx-Engels Reader*, 2nd ed. Edited by Robert Tucker, 146–200. New York: W. W. Norton, 1978.

Millett, Kate. *Sexual Politics*. New York: Ballantine Books, 1987.

Mitchell, Juliette. *Psychoanalysis and Feminism*. New York: Pantheon Books, 1974.

The Negro Family: The Case For National Action. U.S. Department of Labor, Office Policy Planning and Research Staff. Greenwood, Conn.: Greenwood Press, 1981.

Phelan, Shane. *Identity Politics: Lesbian Feminism and the Limits of Community.* Philadelphia: Temple University Press, 1989.

Réage, Pauline. *The Story of O.* New York: Ballantine Books, 1984.

Rebeta-Burditt, Joyce. *The Cracker Factory.* New York: Macmillan, 1977.

Said, Edward. *Orientalism.* New York: Vintage Books, 1979.

Schor, Juliet. *The Overworked America: The Unexpected Decline of Leisure.* New York: Basic Books, 1991.

Scott, Paul. *The Jewel in the Crown.* New York: Avon Books, 1979.

Soble, Alan. *Pornography: Marxism, Feminism, and the Future of Sexuality.* New Haven: Yale University Press, 1986.

Sontag, Susan. "The Pornographic Imagination." In *A Susan Sontag Reader*, 205–33. New York: Farrar, Straus & Giroux, 1982.

Stern, Daniel. *The Interpersonal World of the Infant: A View from Psychoanalysis and Developmental Psychology.* New York: Basic Books, 1985.

Stanton, Domna. "Difference on Trial: A Critique of the Maternal Metaphor in Cixous, Irigaray, and Kristeva." In *The Poetics of Gender.* Edited by Nancy K. Miller, 157–82. New York: Columbia University Press, 1986.

Thigpen, Corbett, and Hervey M. Cleckley. *The Three Faces of Eve.* Kingsport: Arcata Graphics, 1992.

Waugh, Evelyn. *Brideshead Revisited: The Sacred and Profane Memoirs of Captain Charles Ryder.* Boston: Little, Brown, 1945.

Williams, Linda. *Hard Core: Power, Pleasure, and the "Frenzy of the Visible."* Berkeley: University of California Press, 1989.

Woolf, Virginia. *A Room of One's Own.* San Diego: Harcourt Brace Jovanovich, 1990.

Zerilli, Linda. "Rememoration or War? French Feminist Narrative and the Politics of Self-Representation." In *differences: A Journal of Feminist Cultural Studies* 3 (Spring 1991): 1–19.

Index

About the Author

Mary Caputi is trained in political theory, with a specialization in feminist theory. She has taught at Colby College, and now holds a position at Saint Mary's college, Notre Dame. She has published several articles analyzing the relationship between feminism, psychoanalysis, and postmodernism. She is currently working on a project that synthesizes psychoanalytic feminism and critical theory. This is her first book.